Living Sermons
Inspiring Stories for the Soul

Charles E. Cravey

In His Steps Publishing

ISBN: 978-1-58535-012-4 (Print)

ISBN: 978-1-58535-013-1 (EPUB)

Library of Congress Control Number: 202590184

Cravey, Charles E.
Living Sermons: Inspiring Stories for the Soul. 1st ed.
In His Steps Publishing, 2025.
274 pages.
LCCN: 2025901840
Call Number: 252 CRA

The King James Version of the Holy Bible provides all Scriptures.

Cover art by Book Brush (bookbrush.com)

IN HIS STEPS PUBLISHING: Statesboro, Georgia, USA

Contents

Introduction

In a world where we often seek to find peace and wisdom in the middle of the noise of everyday life, comes "Living Sermons" as a glimmer of light and knowledge. This book of inspirational short stories is the real-life story of the triumph of the human spirit, of faith, of resilience, and of compassion. Each of the narratives in this book is a glorious reminder that some of the biggest life-changing moments hide in the most unlikely of places. From a wide range of voices and experiences, "Living Sermons" calls you to a journey of reflection and growth.

Whether it is in your everyday journey or in your quest for purpose, these stories will be your source of inspiration and guidance. As you turn the pages, may you find the courage to face your challenges, the audacity to transform your life, and the wisdom to recognize the beauty of life's simple moments.

Come into a world where stories are alive, where every page is a sermon, and every reader is a witness to the miracles of life. Join me on this journey, and may blessings be upon you.

Charles E. Cravey, February 2025

Foreword

We often envision our life journey as a straight, direct path. But, as we all know, life is anything but—instead, it's a patch of unexpected twists and turns, a group of both good and bad moments that define who we are. This book was created to share stories that represent the diversity of the human experience. Each of the short stories in this book is a testament to the strength, the faith, and the courage that lie in every soul. From the everyday to the extraordinary, these stories capture what it means to stand strong, to have faith, and to win.

In these stories, you will meet people who, through their own private struggles, have become stronger and more courageous. These are not just stories; they are mirrors that reveal the possible greatness in every person.

Find encouragement in these narratives; they remind you of your capacity to conquer obstacles and realize your ambitions. This book is a tribute to the spirit of man, to those people who still have the heart to hope, the will to strive, and the mind to achieve.

Here is a world where every failure is an opportunity for a comeback, and every end is a new beginning. We hope you find as much happiness and inspiration in these stories as we did.

Editor: IN HIS STEPS PUBLISHING

Dedication

I affectionately dedicate this book
to my beloved
First United Methodist Church family
of Statesboro, Georgia.
You have warmly welcomed my family
into your family. May God continue to bless you.

The Rev. Dr. Charles E. Cravey

1

Sin and Clorox

T here is a small village called Serenity Falls on top of the hills, near the streams that make soothing sounds. An ancient church stood there, with its weathered stone walls and Gothic architecture, giving it a mysterious and grand appearance. Its stained-glass windows, depicting biblical scenes, and its beautiful, ornate altar, where many confessed and prayed, made the church famous. Living in the village, the people treasured their strong religious faith and considered the church a sanctuary, a holy place where they could go to confess and wash away their sins. They went to its sacred space to find solace and redemption and to believe that forgiveness was possible.

Among the villagers, there was a man named Samuel; his face was a map of experience and years. He was well thought of by his fellow townspeople because of his kind heart and gentle nature. But this man carried a burden—the burden of a troubled past that pursued him day and night. He had made his choices, and in doing so, he felt unworthy of love and acceptance.

Despite his efforts to change and make amends, the weight of his sins clung to him like the color that does not come out of the cloth. Every day, Samuel walks along the cobblestone streets of Serenity Falls, searching for solace and redemption in the ancient church.

It was evening, and the sun had set below the horizon, casting a golden color to the village. The century-old stone church boasts towers that seem to reach up to the sky in a majestic silhouette as the light fades. With a sense of reverence, Samuel stepped inside; the heavy wooden doors creaked at his touch. A cool air of sacred space caressed him and transported him to a state of tranquility and solace.

As he made his way to the front of the church, the marble floor beneath his footsteps gave a light echo. The sound, however, was harmonious with the whispers of the past. The flickering of the candlelight on the polished pews cast ethereal shadows that seemed to dance coordinated with his thoughts. He reached the altar and kneeled; head bowed in silent prayer. The soft creak of the doors broke the peaceful silence of the church. Samuel looked up, and his eyes met those of Agnes, a much-loved figure in the village. Agnes is the village healer and is renowned for her wisdom and gentle nature. In her hand, she carries a small, unassuming bottle of Clorox bleach.

Curiosity intrigued Samuel as he watched Agnes approach. A sense of anticipation hung heavy in the air, as though a momentous revelation was imminent. An encounter with Agnes and the bleach would transform an ordinary life to an extraordinary one in ways they could not have imagined.

"Samuel," she said with a gentle yet firm voice. "Removing the stains of our past can be difficult, but it is possible. Just as Clorox cleanses and purifies, so can we find redemption and forgiveness."

Agnes, the wise and compassionate village elder, led Samuel to the grandeur of the church's baptismal font. An ethereal silence pervaded the room. Agnes poured a bit of bleach into the water, creating a solution that shimmered like liquid light and illuminated the sacred space.

"This is not just about cleansing the surface, Samuel, but about purifying the soul," she explained with words that carry a weight of significant wisdom. With reverence, Agnes and Samuel dipped their hands into the water, and the coolness of the water seeped into their skin. The touch of the water was both soothing and invigorating, and it was as if it held a secret power to heal and restore. As they washed their hands, the symbolic act became a spiritual journey—a journey of repentance and renewal.

The Clorox water washed away Samuel's grime, and it washed away the guilt and regret that had burdened him for so long. Each droplet that fell from his hands carried with it a piece of his burden, and it dissolved in the depths of the baptismal font. His past—which had once been so stubborn, so indelible—was disappearing, replaced by a sense of liberation, of hope.

In that hallowed moment, Agnes and Samuel understood the true essence of forgiveness. It was not just a matter of removing stains, but a metaphorical process that allowed one to acknowledge their imperfections, learn from their mistakes, and move forward with greater strength and wisdom. That water with Clorox in it was a symbol of purification and redemption, and it enabled their spirits to let go of the past and to begin a new chapter.

As Samuel raised his cleansed hands towards the heavens, an intense sense of gratitude washed over him. He felt the weight that had burdened his soul for so long disappear, and in its place, he felt a deep sense of peace and acceptance. Agnes stood beside him; her eyes filled with pride for Samuel's courage in confronting his demons.

Within the church's quiet, Samuel and Agnes found the power of forgiveness and its potential to transform. Though marred by past mistakes, they found redemption through Clorox and determination. They chose a brighter future.

The cleansing ritual was ongoing, and into the future, Samuel felt a deep sense of peace and liberation. He felt the weight of his sins lift, and in its place, hope and clarity emerged. He realized that forgiveness was not something to be earned, but something to be received.

When the ritual was complete, Agnes, the wise and compassionate village elder, smiled warmly and placed her gentle hand on Samuel's shoulder. "Remember, Samuel," she said in her soothing voice, "true cleansing comes from within. Let go of your past and embrace the present with a heart full of grace and love."

Samuel, a humble and remorseful man, nodded gratefully, absorbing her wisdom. He left the quaint village church that evening feeling lighter; his spirit renewed.

The night air was crisp, carrying the scent of blooming flowers and the muted murmurs of the night. No longer burdened by the weight of his past transgressions, but uplifted by the promise of a brighter future, Samuel walked through the cobblestone streets.

Looking up at the starry sky, he felt an overwhelming sense of awe and gratitude. The twinkling lights above seemed to dance with joy as though they were celebrating his redemption. He knew, deep within his soul, that the light above had washed away the stains of sin and left him pure and radiant. He vowed to live a life of compassion, forgiveness, and love from that moment forward, to cherish the gift of renewal that he had received.

2

Ole Betsy and Enduring Spirits

—◦◦◦—

In a small rural town in the heart of the 1950s South, a young boy named Timmy, and an old man named Gus lived. A wise and weathered farmer, Gus had spent his entire life working the land. His farm, which he tended with great love and care, was in a region of rolling hills and vibrant green pastures. With each passing season, Gus relied on his help from his trusty companion, Betsy, an aging mule who was part of his farming routine.

Betsy, a worn and weary mule, had been with Gus through it all. They had weathered droughts, floods, and long hours of arduous work together. Their bond ran deep, a connection forged from years of shared experiences and mutual dependence. Gus often marveled at the silent understanding between them, a language of trust with no words, just friendship.

It was on one scorching summer day that a young boy named Timmy caught Gus's eye. Timmy, a curious boy with an admiration for the old farmer, Gus, would often find himself in Gus's fields. He would stand at the edge of the field and watch Gus and Betsy. He would watch the rhythmic movements of them working in the blistering sun.

Gus, sensing the boy's interest, invited him over. Timmy hesitated for a moment, his eyes wide with a mix of excitement and nervousness. It was a dream come true for him to be invited into the world of farming by the man he looked up to most. With a twinkle in his eye, Gus asked Timmy, "You ever plow a field?" The boy shook his head, his anticipation growing by the second.

"Well, today's your lucky day," exclaimed Gus, a warm smile spreading across his weathered face. "Betsy and I could sure use an extra pair of hands. Don't worry, she'll show you the ropes." With that, he patted the mule affectionately, repeating the unspoken bond between them.

For Timmy, that sizzling summer day marked the beginning of a new chapter in his life. He began a journey of learning and growth under the tutelage of Gus's wisdom and Betsy's spirit.

Gus handed Timmy the reins of the plow, a sturdy leather contraption that had been in Gus's family for generations. Betsy, a large black mule with a gentle demeanor, pulled the plow. Timmy, a young and eager 12-year-old apprentice, had been watching Gus do the job for weeks, and now it was his turn to try.

As Timmy held the reins, he could feel the weight of responsibility on his shoulders. The sun beat down mercilessly, increasing his nerves. His hands trembled as he struggled to steady them, not knowing if he could do such an important task.

But Gus, a weathered farmer with a kind heart, stood right beside Timmy, giving guidance and encouragement. With every step, Gus told Timmy how to keep a steady pace and align himself properly. Betsy, sensing Timmy's unease, seemed like she knew what was happening and was acting wisely.

As they plowed through the fertile soil, Gus shared stories of his own youth, tales of hard work and perseverance. He told of the lessons he had learned from the land, of the importance of working in tune with nature and its rhythms and cycles. Timmy listened with wide eyes, eager to soak up every bit of wisdom Gus was offering.

The hours passed, but Timmy's determination only grew stronger. Each furrow they created transformed the soil into a canvas ready for new life. And with every passing minute, Timmy's once-shaky hands were becoming steady, guided by a growing confidence.

Through their shared labor, Timmy understood the value of hard work and patience. He learned that actual strength doesn't come from overpowering nature, but from working within it. The lessons that Gus had imparted, just like seeds planted in the fertile soil of Timmy's mind, would grow and make him into a strong and wise farmer.

As the sun set, casting a golden glow over the fields, Timmy and Gus finished their work. The land plowed and ready for planting was their achievement. With a sense of accomplishment and gratitude, Timmy thanked Gus for the valuable lessons he had received from him that day.

As they walked back to the farmhouse, the plow behind them, Timmy couldn't help but feel a deep connection to the land. Gus's guidance would help him work the land and himself. He would be a caretaker of the earth like Gus.

When the day's work was done, Gus, with weathered hands and a heart of gold, looked at Timmy, his young apprentice, with pride. The two had spent the entire day working under the scorching sun, tending to the land that had been in Gus's family for generations. Sweat dripped from their brows, but their spirits remained high because they were driven by their passion for the land and a deep connection to their ancestors.

"You've done good, son," Gus said, his voice filled with admiration and parental warmth. "Remember, the land rewards those who treat it with respect, just as life rewards those who face it with courage and determination."

Timmy nodded, his eyes shining with gratitude and a newfound sense of purpose. He had always looked up to Gus not only for his farming skills but also for his integrity and wisdom. In working side by side, Gus had taught Timmy the importance of hard work, perseverance, and humility during their day together.

The sun set, casting a golden color across the vast field. Gus, Timmy, and Betsy had formed a harmonious trio to represent the bond between man, boy, and beast through the years. At that moment, the world seemed to come to a standstill to recognize the beauty of their unity and the significance of their work.

Their dedication and care had tilled the land that was once just soil and nurtured into life. Every seed they planted, every weed they pulled, helped to enrich the earth, bringing forth the crops that would feed their community. It was a humbling realization for Timmy, who now understood that they were not just growing food but discharging the responsibility to maintain and protect the land for future generations.

As the gentle breeze whispered through the trees, whispering the wisdom of creation, Timmy couldn't help but feel grateful. He knew that the lessons of his days, the wisdom of his ancestors, would be the foundation upon which he would build his life. Guided by the land and taught by Gus and Betsy, Timmy set out on a journey of self-discovery, fueled by a respect for the earth and a desire to make a positive change. He promised Gus that he would return.

As the sun dipped below the horizon, the sky became violet and purple. Gus, Timmy, and Betsy stood together; their figures silhouetted against the fertile land. It was a powerful and touching moment that spoke of the enduring power of hard work, wisdom, and friendship between a man, a boy, and a mule. Together, they were a testament to the indomitable spirit of those who work the land and, in doing so, shape their own futures and the world around them.

3

The Keeper of Memories

⊸⟐⊷

Deep within the Georgia woods where tall pine trees stood and the scent of earth filled the air, there was just a modest shack. This humble abode had seen better days, but to the aged man living within it, it was a sanctuary of love and memories. An old dog, Max, a loyal Labrador Retriever with a graying muzzle, was his only constant companion.

The shack is where Henry has lived his whole life, it seems. It has been his sanctuary from the chaos of the world, a place where he found peace and solace. The shack, situated amid the lush greenery, has withstood countless storms and changing of seasons. The story of a simpler time is told through its worn and faded wooden walls.

Inside, the modest furniture and rustic decor exudes a sense of warmth and nostalgia. The fireplace, adorned with family photos and trinkets collected over the years, provides both heat and a comforting ambiance.

Henry would rise with the sun, his steps slow and deliberate as he made his way to the creaky wooden porch. He carried a steaming cup of coffee in his hand and settled into a worn rocking chair. Its rhythmic creaks echoed through the stillness of the forest. From this vantage point, Henry watched as nature stirred to life. The gentle rustling of leaves and the melodic chirping of birds filled his ears. Max would lie at his feet, his tail wagging lazily as he enjoys the serenity of the forest.

As the day unfolded, Henry would often venture into the surrounding woods, traversing well-worn paths and exploring hidden nooks. He would lose himself in the solitude, finding solace in the symphony of nature's sounds. Occasionally, he would stumble upon a patch of wildflowers, their vibrant hues a stark contrast against the muted earth tones of the forest floor. With a smile, he would pick a few blossoms and carefully tuck them into the pocket of his weathered jacket, a simple reminder of the beauty that surrounded him.

Henry and Max spent their evenings around the crackling fireplace. Max would tell stories and reminisce about days gone by. The flickering flames danced across their weathered faces, casting a soft glow inside the room. Henry's laugh resonated through the air; a melodic sound that rang with the joy he found in the simplicity of life.

In this humble shack, within the Georgia woods, Henry had found his haven. It was a place where time stood still, where the worries and chaos of the world seemed distant and inconsequential. Surrounded by the beauty of nature and the unwavering companionship of Max, Henry had discovered a peace that eluded him elsewhere.

As he settled into his worn armchair each night, he couldn't help but feel grateful for the humble shack that had become his sanctuary, his refuge from the world outside. Henry often shared his stories with Max as if the dog could understand every word.

"You know, Max," he would say, "this old shack has seen a lot. It was here that I met your mother, a beautiful golden retriever named Daisy. We used to run through these woods, chasing after rabbits and playing in the stream. Those were some of the best days of my life." Max would look up at Henry with his soulful eyes, like he acknowledges the stories and found enjoyment in the memories just as much as his master does. They have shared many moments, from Max as that rambunctious puppy chewing on Henry's boots to the old dog he is now, only wanting to be near Henry.

As Henry continued to share his stories, the cozy old shack became a time capsule of their adventures. Faded photographs on the walls captured the joy and laughter they had experienced through the years. Every photograph told a story of their deep bond —— from hiking trips in the mountains to lazy afternoons spent napping under the shade of a tree. The nearby stream and the wooded area's scent filled the shack; it reminded them of happier times.

Max has been a loyal companion since the moment he entered Henry's life. His mischievous antics as a puppy brought laughter and warmth to their home when he chewed on Henry's boots or dug up the flower beds. As Max grew older, his energy waned, but his love for Henry never wavered. He had become a wise and gentle old dog, content with just being by Henry's side, offering comfort and companionship in the twilight of their years. The quiet old shack held many reflective moments for Henry and Max.

There, they cherished their memories and felt gratitude for their experiences. The bond they had formed went beyond words, as if they could communicate through a language of love and understanding that transcended the limitations of speech. Henry cherished the time spent with Max in their beloved old shack; Max's presence was a constant reminder of a loyal companion's unconditional love and joy.

One crisp fall morning, Henry took Max on a walk through the woods. It was a rare day when Henry felt energetic, and Max's ears perked up with excitement as they set off on their adventure. People knew the forest on the outskirts of their small town for its breathtaking beauty during fall.

As they ventured deeper into the woods, the trees stood tall and proud, displaying their bright reds, oranges, and yellows. The fallen leaves covered the ground, and they crunched satisfyingly under their feet as they wandered along the familiar trails. As they walked, Henry's thoughts drifted to a time many years ago when he had first come to these woods. It was a time of healing and solace, a period right after the war when Henry was grappling with the traumas and hardships he had endured.

"This place was my sanctuary after the war," he said, his voice tinged with nostalgia. "I built this shack with my own hands, using whatever materials I could find. It wasn't much, but it was home." He smiled as he reminisced about the countless hours he had spent restoring the shack, turning it into a cozy refuge where he could escape the outside world and find peace within himself.

They continued their leisurely stroll until they reached a clearing where a small stream trickled gently. The sound of water dancing over rocks was soothing to their ears, providing a moment of tranquility amidst the rustling leaves.

Henry took a break and sat down on a fallen log, his weathered hands resting on his knees. Max, ever the faithful companion, settled beside him, leaning into his side. The bond between man and dog was palpable, their connection forged through countless adventures and shared experiences. Mischief twinkled in Henry's eyes as he turned to Max.

"Remember that fishing trip we took here?" he asked. His voice carried a warm chuckle, echoing through the muted clearing. "You were just a pup then, and you jumped into the water, trying to catch the fish with your paws. I laughed so hard that day, Max. You sure know how to make me smile." Max wagged his tail in response, as if understanding the sentiment behind Henry's words.

As the sun filtered through the trees, casting dappled shadows on their surroundings, Henry and Max sat there, basking in the moment's serenity. The woods were Henry's sanctuary. Now, man and dog find refuge there, displaying the strength of nature and their companionship. Max's tail thumped against the ground, and he licked Henry's hand as if to say, "I remember too." The bond between them was unspoken, yet profound, a testament to the years they had spent together.

As the sun set, casting a golden glow over the forest, they made their way back to the shack. The evening air was cool, and Henry wrapped a blanket around his shoulders, feeling the weight of his years. Max lay at his feet, his presence a comforting warmth. Henry knew that time was slipping away, but he found solace in the memories they had created.

Throughout their lives, Henry and Max had shared countless adventures in the woods surrounding their small rustic shack. The towering trees and babbling brooks had witnessed their laughter, their tears, and their triumphs. From their early days together, when Max was just a playful pup, to their more recent years of quiet companionship, their connection had only grown stronger. The woods had been their sanctuary, a place where they could escape the hustle and bustle of everyday life.

Henry had taught Max to navigate the winding trails, their footprints etched into the earth as a testament to their explorations. Together, they had discovered hidden clearings, stumbled upon breathtaking waterfalls, and marveled at the beauty of nature in its purest form.

As the years passed, the shack became a symbol of their shared memories. Its weathered walls told the story of countless storms weathered and peaceful nights spent under the starry sky. Now, with Henry feeling the weight of his years, he found solace in the simple pleasures of their routine.

Each evening, as the sun set, they would return to the shack, their weary bodies finding comfort in its humble embrace. The warmth of the crackling fire would fill the air, and Max would curl up at Henry's feet. As the twilight hours enveloped them, Henry would reflect on the richness of their shared experiences. The countless walks through the woods, the playful games of fetch, the quiet moments of contemplation–they all formed the tapestry of a life well-lived. Expressing gratitude for their bond, Henry gently stroked Max's fur, acknowledging the immense joy and love woven into their lives.

In the twilight of their time together, Henry and Max found solace and contentment in their old shack, nestled in the embrace of the woods. The memories they had created were priceless treasures, far more valuable than any worldly possession.

As Henry whispered his gratitude for their shared moments, he knew he would forever cherish these memories in his heart, a testament to their enduring bond. Max rested his head on Henry's lap, his eyes closing in contentment. In the twilight of their lives, they found peace in each other's company, knowing that their bond would endure even as the world around them changed.

And so, in that little shack in the woods, an aged man and his loyal old dog continued to share their days, creating recent memories while cherishing the old. For as long as they had each other, they knew they were never truly alone.

4

Threads of Kindness

⸺❖⸺

In the village of Waverly, between the rivers and the rolling hills, lived Megan, a home-based seamstress. At fifty, Megan had the wisdom of age combined with the vitality of someone much younger. Her life was simple and unassuming, but her heart was a treasure trove of kindness.

Her home was a charming, thatched-roof cottage on the outskirts of the village, adorned with blooming flowers and vines climbing the walls. It was a pretty sight—the cottage and its colorful window shutters. Megan's sewing studio held piles of fabric and spools of thread, bathed in sunlight and warmth. Here, she spent her days working diligently at her sewing machine, making beautiful garments and mending tattered clothes for the villagers. With precision, she moved her practiced hands.

Megan has filled her studio walls with colorful fabrics over the years; each tells a story. Although she leads a modest lifestyle, her impact on the community is profound. She has a way of making everyone feel special. She is interested in their lives, and she will help when needed. Whether it was altering a dress for a young girl to attend her first dance or repairing a tear in someone's much loved jacket, Megan's kindness knew no bounds. Megan always performed acts of kindness quietly and consistently, such as the gentle hum of her sewing machine outside her cottage.

The villagers would often visit her, not only for their clothing needs but also to get a dose of Megan's warm smile and comforting presence. She was a pillar of strength and compassion, always ready to lend an ear or offer a word of encouragement. Megan can mend clothes, but it's her capacity to mend hearts and lift spirits that makes her truly extraordinary.

In the village of Waverly, Megan was more than just a seamstress. She was a beacon of light, stitching together the fabric of the community with love and kindness.

It was on a chilly winter evening the previous year that Mrs. Harris, a widow, came to see Megan. Since her husband's death, Mrs. Harris has struggled financially. Now, she battled the harsh elements in a dilapidated coat, its worn fabric a testament to her difficult circumstances.

Without a moment's hesitation, Megan invited her in, served her a cup of warm tea, and started on the coat. The fire crackled merrily. In its warm glow, Mrs. Harris recounted tales of her youth while Megan, her needle flying, mended the damaged cloth. Every stitch that Megan made with her skilled hands was bringing the coat back to its former glory, fixing the frayed edges and strengthening the weak points.

Megan's generosity, however, did not stop there. Having listened to the tales of Mrs. Harris's youth, she added a touch of beauty to the coat. With delicate embroidery, Megan adorned the once plain garment with intricate patterns to represent the strength and resilience of Mrs. Harris.

As the evening ended, the coat that Megan had altered looked amazing on Mrs. Harris. Tears of gratitude appeared in her eyes as she thanked Megan. Megan smiled and told her it was okay. She knew she had done more than just warm the coat; she had also warmed Mrs. Harris's heart a little.

At night, when Megan was cleaning her sewing room, she felt satisfied with her work. It's not just physical warmth that the act of repairing and embellishing Mrs. Harris's coat brought, but it also kindled hope and companionship in their hearts. Megan realized that there is a lot of power in minor acts of kindness, and they can have a lasting impact on people's lives. Megan's generosity went beyond her talent in sewing because she also had an eye for those in need and could create beautiful garments and accessories.

On another occasion, while working diligently in her cozy cottage, Megan couldn't help but notice a young boy named Tommy. He would often stand outside her window; his eyes would widen with curiosity and longing. It was clear to Megan that Tommy came from a poor family because his clothes were always dirty and tattered.

One day, Megan acted and called Tommy to her cottage and asked the young boy if he would like to learn to sew. The eyes of the young boy lit up at the offer, and he agreed to Megan's invitation right away.

From that moment on, Tommy visited Megan regularly in her humble home, and she taught him sewing. Under the guidance of Megan, who was very compassionate and a wonderful teacher, Tommy showed talent in sewing. He made insignificant items like little stuffed animals and hand-sewn pouches and took them home to show his family.

As time passed, Megan and Tommy became not just teacher and student but friends whose bond was based on love and the enjoyment of creating things. Megan saw in Tommy a potential for a successful future, and she wanted to help him achieve it. She did not see the present circumstances, and she knew that with the right support and encouragement, he could overcome any obstacle.

Through their shared interest in sewing, Megan was not only teaching Tommy a skill but also giving him hope and confidence in himself. They were stitching together a beautiful tale of resilience, kindness, and the power of generosity with every stitch they made.

Over the years, Megan has become the symbol of compassion and generosity in Waverly because she has always been there to help the people in need. She has always been active in the community and is involved in many charitable activities. From food drives to clothing for the needy, Megan has always been willing to lend a helping hand.

Not only did she work on extensive projects, but Megan also found joy in the small acts of service. She would spend hours making sure that every stitch was perfect as she fixed the town's festival banners. Everyone in Waverly knew about her attention to detail and her dedication to preserving the traditions of the town.

However, it was Megan's talent and passion for fashion that made her stand out. Recognizing that many of the brides in the area did not have the financial resources to purchase their wedding dresses, she put her sewing skills to use. With love and care, she created beautiful wedding dresses for these brides. These unique creations made not only the brides happy but also became family heirlooms that the brides passed on to their children and grandchildren.

Megan's cottage was a home not only to her but to all those in need. It served as a place of refuge for all of them. Many people knew Megan as a kind and gentle soul, and they all sought her counsel and support in times of difficulty.

Although Megan's life may not be filled with grand achievements or worldwide recognition, she touched Waverly and its people positively. Her legacy lives on. It's in the hearts of those she touched, the clothes she mended, and the smiles of the villagers who knew her. Kindness and dedication have always been the strength of Megan and will always inspire the community to help each other, no matter how long she has been gone.

5

The Colors of Freedom

He has always known his destiny was to create. As a child, he found comfort in the gentle stroke of the brush across the canvas and the wonderful array of colors before him. To create art brought him a feeling of fulfillment that nothing else could touch. But as an adult, he found himself stuck in a nine-to-five job at a dull office. The monotony of his daily existence extinguished the creative spark that once burned so brightly within him.

His art supplies, which had at one time been so vibrant and inviting, now sit untouched and covered in dust in the corner of his small apartment. The colors that once brought such vibrancy to his art had faded, almost mirroring the loss of passion in Roger's heart. Each day, he would stare longingly at the untouched canvas, wishing to pick up his brushes and let his imagination run wild once again. But the weight of responsibility, not to mention the fear of failure, holds him back, keeping him stuck in a life devoid of purpose.

One rainy afternoon, on his way home from another uninspiring day at work, he stumbles upon a small art gallery hidden away on a quiet street. The sign above the door reads "Roberson's Gallery." Curious about the unknown, Roger's curiosity gets the better of him, and he steps inside.

The moment he steps across the threshold, Roger feels a wave of tranquility wash over him. The scent of fresh paint and the hum of conversation fill the air. An eclectic mix of artwork adorns the walls, each piece its own storytelling. It is as if the gallery itself is alive, breathing with creativity and possibility.

In that moment, Roger knows he has found his sanctuary. The gallery has become his refuge from the monotonous downpour of his everyday life; a place where he can escape from his own reality and become immersed in the world of art. He spends hours wandering the halls, studying the brushstrokes and the colors on the canvases. It is here that Roger discovers his passion again, the flame within him burning brightly with a renewed intensity.

Inspired by the talent and creativity displayed, Roger makes a bold decision. He will no longer allow himself to be confined by the shackles of a mundane job that crushes his artistic spirit. He will reclaim his identity as a creator and pursue his passion without reserve.

With renewed determination, he sets out to dust off his own art supplies, ready to breathe new life into his neglected canvas. Roberson's Gallery has become more than just a place of escape for Roger; it has become the catalyst for a life-changing journey. It is within these hallowed walls he finds the courage to take the first step towards a life of purpose and fulfillment. The gallery will now be his sanctuary, a haven where his dreams can take flight and where he can at last answer his call as an artist.

Inside the gallery, the air is thick with the smell of oil paint and varnish, an intoxicating atmosphere that envelops the space. The soft lighting enhances the vivid colors and the intricate details of the artworks, and they capture the senses of all who enter. Roger, an art enthusiast, wanders through the aisles, his eyes wide with wonder, taking in the beautiful works on the walls. Each piece of art tells a story bursting with emotion and a vivid depiction of life. The brushstrokes dance across the canvases, demonstrating the artist's technical skill and unique perspective.

As he reaches the back of the gallery, Roger notices an aged man with a shock of white hair standing in front of an easel enveloped in his painting. The man's hands move with an almost supernatural grace, as if he is effortlessly bringing his vision to life stroke by stroke. Roger can't help but feel a pang of envy towards the artist and his undeniable talent and dedication.

However, mixed with the envy is a flicker of hope, a spark of inspiration that ignites within him. With a mix of nervousness and admiration, Roger approaches the aged man, interrupting his artistic trance. The man looks up, his piercing blue eyes meeting Roger's, eyes that reflect years of experience and wisdom. Encouraged by his admiration, Roger speaks hesitantly, staring his awe at the incredible work before him. With a humble smile, the aged man nods, confirming that he is indeed Mr. Roberson, the mastermind behind these captivating creations.

The man smiles warmly, setting his brush down. "Yes, I am. And you are?"

"Roger. I'm an artist too, or at least I used to be," Roger replied, feeling a rush of emotions. "But I feel stuck, lost in a job that drains all my creativity." Mr. Roberson's eyes soften with understanding.

"Ah, the plight of many artists. It's easy to lose ourselves in the demands of the world and forget the passion that once drove us. But remember, Roger, art is not just a profession; it's a calling, a way of life."

The two men talk for hours, telling stories and discussing the nuances of the craft. Mr. Roberson recounts his journey as an artist, the struggles and triumphs, the low points, and the high points. He spoke of the times when he wanted to give up, when the weight of society's expectations threatened to drown his creative spirit. But amidst the challenges, Mr. Roberson found solace in the power of art. He shared how he rediscovered his true purpose by immersing himself in the process of creation, focusing on the joy and fulfillment it brought him. He emphasized the importance of staying true to oneself as an artist, never compromising on one's artistic integrity.

As the conversation progressed, Mr. Roberson offered Roger practical advice on finding a balance between his day job and his artistic pursuits. He suggested setting aside dedicated time each day to nurture his creative side, whether it be through sketching, painting, or simply observing the world around him with a discerning eye.

Feeling inspired, Roger soaked in every word, his passion reigniting like a dormant flame. Mr. Roberson's words of encouragement resonated deeply within him, reminding him of the deep-seated love he had for art.

Before parting ways, Mr. Roberson invited Roger to return to the gallery whenever he wished, admire the artwork, and be an active part of the creative process. The gallery would be Roger's sanctuary, a place where he could freely express himself and rediscover the joy of creation.

With gratitude in his heart, Roger bid Mr. Roberson farewell, feeling a renewed sense of purpose and determination. He knew that from that moment on, he would no longer allow his job to stifle his artistic spirit. He was ready to embrace his true calling and embark on a journey of self-discovery through his art.

Days turned into weeks, and Roger spent every spare moment at Roberson's Gallery. Under the expert guidance and mentorship of Mr. Roberson, Roger tirelessly honed his skills and experimented with various techniques. Through countless hours of experimentation, he discovered his unique voice as an artist, infusing his work with a captivating blend of emotion and creativity.

As his confidence grew, so did his body of work, with each new piece reflecting his artistic growth and evolution. One evening, as Roger carefully applied the final brushstrokes to a challenging piece, Mr. Roberson approached him with an expression of profound pride. His eyes sparkled with excitement as he shared his belief in Roger's talent.

"Roger, my dear boy, I believe it's time for you to share your extraordinary gift with the world," he declared, his voice filled with genuine admiration. "I will proudly host your first solo exhibition here at the gallery."

Roger's heart raced with a mix of anticipation and trepidation. This invitation was his breakthrough. It gave him the chance to leave his boring job and finally pursue his art. The prospect of displaying his work in a renowned gallery was both exhilarating and daunting. This opportunity exposed his innermost thoughts and emotions to the scrutiny of others, yet it also offered a chance to connect with kindred spirits who might appreciate his creations.

As Roger stood before Mr. Roberson, gratitude and determination welled up within him. He knew that accepting this offer would require immense dedication and sacrifice, but he also understood that it was an opportunity that must not be squandered.

With newfound resolve, he looked into Mr. Roberson's eyes and replied, "Thank you, sir. I am ready to take this leap of faith and share my art with the world. Let's make this exhibition a celebration of creativity and self-expression."

And so, with the support and guidance of his mentor, Roger began an intensive journey of preparation and self-discovery. He poured his heart and soul into each piece, meticulously selecting the artworks that would best represent his artistic vision. The gallery walls became his canvas, and the anticipation of the upcoming exhibition fueled his creative fire.

As the date of the solo exhibition approached, Roger's excitement mingled with a touch of nervousness. He understood this event would serve as a pivotal moment in his artistic career, a chance to introduce himself to the world as a serious artist. Yet, he also knew that he had worked tirelessly,

pushing his boundaries, and striving for excellence. With unwavering determination and a profound belief in his abilities, Roger eagerly awaited
the unveiling of his artistic journey to the world.

The night of the long-awaited exhibition arrived, and the prestigious
gallery was abuzz with anticipation. Roger's meticulously crafted artwork
adorned the walls, each piece a testament to his unwavering dedication and
artistic vision. As he stood amidst the crowd, his heart pounded with a
blend of nervousness and excitement.

The visitors, clad in their finest attire, moved gracefully from one artwork to another, their eyes captivated by the exquisite beauty and raw
emotions emanating from Roger's creations. Roger, a once lost soul
searching for meaning, now stood tall, his doubts and insecurities fading
away with each passing minute. He had poured his heart and soul into
every stroke of the brush, every stroke telling a story of his personal journey
through darkness and into the light. The emotions that had consumed him
for years were now laid bare on the canvas, inviting viewers to step into his
world, if only for a moment.

As the evening progressed, Roger observed the crowd's reactions, their
expressions mirroring the emotions he had infused into his artwork. He
couldn't help but feel a profound sense of fulfillment and purpose. The
connection between artist and audience was intense, as if the colors and
textures on the canvas had bridged the gap between their souls. It was in
that moment that Roger knew he had found his calling. People finally
heard and understood his voice.

As the exhibition ended, the gallery owner, Mr. Roberson approached
the stage and raised his glass to honor Roger's remarkable talent. The
room fell silent, all eyes fixed on the man who had captured the essence of
freedom within his art.

"To Roger," Mr. Roberson declared, his voice ringing with admiration.

"A talented artist who found his way back to the colors of freedom. May you find endless inspiration and boundless creativity on your journey."

In that moment, he felt an overwhelming warmth spread through his chest. It was a feeling of validation and acceptance, as if the years of doubt and self-questioning had finally been silenced. Roger had found his place in the world, a sanctuary where he could be unapologetically himself and share his passion with others. He basked in the applause, knowing this was just the start of a lifelong artistic journey full of potential. His art would touch many hearts and souls. With renewed determination, Roger embraced the path that lay before him, ready to paint the vibrant tapestry of his future.

Roger's artistic journey started under the tutelage of renowned art professor Mr. Roberson. Mr. Roberson, with his years of experience and deep understanding of the art world, saw the raw talent and passion within Roger and took him under his wing. He became not only a mentor but also a source of inspiration, challenging Roger to push the boundaries of his creativity and to explore new mediums and techniques.

Under Mr. Roberson's guidance, Roger's artistic skills flourished, and he discovered a newfound sense of purpose and fulfillment in his work. The once directionless artist had found his purpose and the freedom to create without limits, as he embarked on a life-changing journey of self-discovery and artistic expression. With each stroke of his brush and every color he blended on his canvas, Roger's art captivated audiences, evoking emotions and sparking conversations.

Roger's growing reputation led to prestigious galleries and exhibitions displaying his artwork. His unique style, characterized by bold brush-strokes and vibrant colors, became his signature, setting him apart from other artists. Roger's dedication and unwavering commitment to his craft earned him numerous accolades and awards, solidifying his position as a rising star in the art world.

Today, Roger continues to evolve as an artist, constantly exploring innovative ideas and pushing the boundaries of his creativity. His artwork continues to inspire and resonate with viewers, leaving an indelible mark on the art community.

As Roger reflects on his journey, he recognizes it was the guidance and support of Mr. Roberson that paved the way for his success. He remains forever grateful for the opportunity to have learned from such a remarkable mentor and teacher. Roger's vibrant tapestry of artistic achievements ensures a future filled with endless possibilities as an acclaimed artist.

6

The Importance of Wood

⚊⊰⊱⚊

One of my pastors, Rev. Lauren West, who is an incredibly talented and inspiring speaker, gave a wonderful sermon at the church last Sunday. The sermon she delivered was quite an interesting one as she talked about the wedding at Cana in Galilee. Rev. West, a knowledgeable and engaging pastor, made her discussion of Jesus' first miracle particularly captivating. Her connection with her congregation was evident. She discussed the significance of this event and the themes of abundance, transformation, and the power of faith. Through her thought-provoking sermon, Rev. West asked us to look at the miracles in our own lives and trust in God's provision for us. Her eloquent delivery and heartfelt message left an impression on all who were present.

Her sermon, however, made me wonder if this was really the first miracle that Jesus ever performed. Looking at the historical and biblical record, there is a gap in our knowledge of Jesus' life from his birth through age 12 and onwards. The Gospels offer a fascinating, albeit limited, perspective on Jesus' public life and miracles. Information about his early years, however, is scarce. This gap leaves one wondering, for instance, what Mary and Joseph, Jesus' devoted parents, were like and how they interpreted the remarkable child that was Jesus. Without concrete evidence, we can only speculate about the possibility of earlier miracles or other extraordinary events that may have contributed to his character and his divine purpose.

My science fiction side makes me think that before turning water into wine, Jesus performed earlier miracles as well. Had he done that before? It's interesting to think about what other extraordinary feats Jesus may have accomplished, even as a child. Could he have healed the sick or even raised the dead? Could he have walked on water or have multiplied food to feed the hungry prior to his adult ministries?

Since we believe Jesus was not just an ordinary man but a divine being with supernatural powers, these questions arise. The water into wine miracle is a glimpse of what Jesus could have done throughout his life. It opens the imagination and the curiosity about the untold miracles that may have occurred both before and after this event. Exploring these ideas allows us to delve deeper into the mysterious and awe-inspiring nature of Jesus' life and teachings.

I recall vividly Pastor Mark Burgess's sermon last week. He told the captivating story of Mary and Joseph's Passover journey to Jerusalem. Their 12-year-old son, Jesus, went with them. However, on their long three-day journey back home, in the middle of the crowd, Jesus was missing. Panicked and worried, Mary and Joseph immediately turned around and hurried back to Jerusalem to look for their beloved child.

It was such an exhausting and anxious journey back to the city; they asked everyone they met if they had seen Jesus. They had been searching for what felt like an eternity when they finally found him in the temple. Mary and Joseph must have felt an overwhelming sense of happiness and relief upon being reunited with their son, knowing that he was safe and unharmed after what had transpired.

But what amazed Mary and Joseph was what they saw in the temple. Not only was Jesus, their little son, sitting there among the priests and elders, he was even engaging with them, teaching them things they had never heard before. It was incredible to witness a 12-year-old boy command so much respect from the religious leaders.

That is why, according to the Gospel of Luke, Mary saved all these things in her heart. It is a wonderful experience to have had Jesus, his wisdom, and his divine presence, and to treasure these memories of him. In the temple, Mary treasured time with her son. She admired his connection to God and his thirst for knowledge, a desire she understood.

This story shows the importance of Jesus' life and mission on Earth. Even at an early age, he displayed wisdom beyond his years and a deep connection to the divine. It also reminds us of the importance of treasuring and reflecting upon the profound moments we experience in our own lives, just as Mary did.

So, you may ask, what was Jesus' life like in those quiet years, also referred to as the "hidden years" or the "lost years"? Well, during this period, Jesus lived an unknown and undocumented life. The Bible states Jesus was born in Bethlehem to Joseph and Mary.

People believe a humble carpenter, Jesus' father, raised Jesus in his house and taught him the trade. He spent most of his early years in Nazareth in Galilee, where people assumed he led a normal life like that of other people in the community. He helped his family, attended the synagogue, took part in community events, and so on. There is extraordinarily little information on Jesus' formative years. Many believe his spiritual growth during this period deepened his understanding of his divine calling, preparing him for his significant role in history.

My science fiction-loving mind wonders if Jesus's early life included displays of God's power since the scriptures only detail his adult ministry. While the Bible doesn't go into detail about Jesus' childhood, it mentions a few key events.

For instance, the Gospel of Luke mentions in brief Jesus' visit to the temple at 12, where he astonished the teachers with his understanding and knowledge. This offers a glimpse of the extraordinary wisdom and spiritual connection Jesus possessed, even from an early age.

The Bible also states that Jesus increased in wisdom and in favor both with God and men, so his divine nature developed continuously during his early years. Imagining God's power and Jesus's influence during his formative years is fascinating, even though the Bible doesn't detail them specifically.

I can just picture a day among fellow students at his Hebrew school and the miraculous things they may have witnessed. The school that Jesus attended was a place of wonder and awe. Every day, his classmates would get together, looking forward to seeing what incredible feats Jesus would perform. He would turn water into wine at lunchtime or heal a sick classmate with just a touch of his hand. The excitement and curiosity of the school were tangible as the students marveled at their peer's extraordinary abilities.

Not only did the students possibly witness his miracles, but Mary and Joseph, his parents, also saw remarkable things in their young child as he grew. From an early age, Jesus displayed wisdom and understanding that were beyond his years. His deep knowledge of the scriptures and the ability to engage in profound theological discussions amazed his parents. They watched with awe as he showed compassion towards others, always desiring to help those in need.

As Jesus grew older, his parents saw an unwavering commitment to his purpose in life. They may have seen him perform countless acts of kindness and compassion, healing the sick, feeding the hungry, and comforting the brokenhearted. Their son's ability to inspire hope and renewal in those who had lost faith amazed Mary and Joseph.

Incredible moments and miraculous encounters characterized the journey of Jesus' life. Whether it was the astonishment of his fellow students at school or the wonder of his parents as they watched him grow, the impact of his presence was undeniable. Jesus' life was a testament to the power of faith and the limitless potential that lies within each of us.

We believe the first miracle is the miracle of turning water into wine; however, we do not know exactly what occurred in the young life of Jesus. We know he was born in Bethlehem to Mary and Joseph.

People believe Jesus learned woodworking from his father and spent most of his early years in the carpenter's shop perfecting his skills. Jesus began his ministry as an adult and performed many miracles and preached about love, forgiveness, and salvation. His earthly life culminated in his crucifixion, where they crucified him on a wooden cross.

Jesus' life, from a carpenter's son to a cross, is such a powerful symbol of his journey and his love for humanity. The importance of wood in this journey is incredibly significant.

7

Lessons from the River

❖

In the small western North Carolina town of Revere, Stephen, a curious boy, felt called to the winding river for no apparent reason. At 12, his heart became tangled with the river, and he loved it, respecting its power with every fiber of his being. But he didn't know that three life-changing encounters with the river's strong currents awaited him.

While meeting the exceptional power of the water, Stephen also encountered his own indomitable spirit and the unbreakable bonds of friendship. His experiences in Revere defined his world view. He discovered his potential and grew in spirit. The town, though tranquil, was also enigmatic.

First Fall: Finding Courage Within

It was a late spring afternoon with a heavy scent of blooming flowers in the air. A thrill-seeker at heart, Stephen couldn't help but go to the nearby river that warm day. The sparkling water called to him, promising an adventure waiting to be had. With a mischievous grin on his face, he climbed out onto a rickety old dock — the weathered wood creaking beneath his weight. He was determined to find the perfect skipping stone, and after a few moments, his eyes landed on a smooth stone nestled between the pebbles. His heart racing with anticipation, he carefully stooped and stretched out his hand to grab it just beneath the water. But fate had other plans. As his fingers grazed the surface of the stone, the old dock beneath him groaned in protest. Without warning, it gave way, sending Stephen plummeting into the icy water below. The shock of the chilly water hitting his body took his breath away, and he gasped for air as he resurfaced.

Adrenaline coursed through his veins, mixing with a sense of exhilaration and a hint of panic. As he clung to the remnants of the broken dock, he couldn't help but marvel at the unexpected turn of events. He did not know that this unplanned dip would be the start of an unforgettable escapade, replete with both challenges and unforgettable memories.

Panic flooded his senses as he struggled to stay afloat, his compact frame battling the current. Visions of his life—his mother's warm embrace, his father's proud smile—flashed before him. Before darkness could claim him, muscular arms pulled him up. It was Ben, his best friend, who had been fishing nearby.

"Gotcha!" Ben said, breathless but grinning. Stephen, his best friend since childhood, had just pulled off a prank that involved a sudden plunge into the river. Gasping for air, Stephen coughed and spluttered but managed a shaky smile. He was safe—for now.

This near-drowning experience had awakened a courage within Stephen, a new determination to face life's challenges head-on. It was as if the intense rush of adrenaline in that moment had unlocked a hidden reservoir of strength and fortitude deep within him. From that day forward, Stephen vowed to embrace every obstacle with unwavering determination and a fearless spirit, knowing that he had the power to overcome any challenge that lay ahead.

As he reflected on the events that had just unfolded, Stephen couldn't help but feel a newfound sense of empowerment. He resolved to approach life with renewed determination. He knew he had the grit to overcome any challenge.

Second Encounter: Discovering Inner Strength

Summer brought sweltering days and the unavoidable allure of swimming. Stephen, a bit more cautious this time, joined his friends at the town's swimming hole at the river. They dared each other to jump from the tallest rock, a daring feat that tested their bravery and pushed their limits.

Despite a gnawing fear, Stephen accepted the challenge, determined to conquer his own apprehensions. The jump was exhilarating, the rush of adrenaline coursing through his veins as he plummeted towards the water below.

However, the impact was harder than he expected, jolting his body and momentarily disorienting him. The shock caused him to lose his bearings, disoriented and struggling to regain control. Down he went, deeper and deeper, as his lungs screamed for air, the weight of the water pressing down on him. Panic set in as he frantically tried to swim back up to the surface, his mind racing with thoughts of survival.

In that terrifying moment, Stephen's life flashed before his eyes once again. He thought of all the adventures still to be had, the places yet to be explored, and the people he had yet to meet. He was about to surrender to the depths, his body weak and his hope fading, when a firm grip around his arm stopped him from going under.

Maria, a classmate and fellow daredevil, had seen him go under and dove in after him without hesitation. With unwavering determination, she propelled herself through the water, her muscles straining against the resistance, until she reached him. With surprising strength, she pulled him to the surface, breaking through the barrier that had threatened to consume him.

Gasping for air, their chests heaving, Stephen and Maria clung to each other, their hearts pounding in sync. In that moment, they felt a bond that transcended their friendship, a connection forged through a shared experience of danger and rescue. Gratitude flooded over Stephen as he realized the immense value of genuine friendship and the lengths to which someone would go to save another.

Together, they swam back to the shore, their bodies tired but their spirits renewed. The swimming hole, once a place of carefree joy, had now become a testament to the strength and determination of the human spirit.

"You should stop scaring us like that," she said, her voice trembling with worry and her eyes wide with concern. Stephen, still catching his breath, nodded in agreement, feeling a mix of gratefulness and humility wash over him.

It was in that moment, as he stood there, his heart still racing, that he realized this encounter had unveiled a strength within him he hadn't known existed. It was a strength that enabled him to rise above adversity, to face his fears head-on, and to push through the darkest of moments.

Third Test: Embracing Resilience

Fall transformed the scenic town of Revere into a breathtaking tapestry of vibrant reds and golds. Stephen and his adventurous group of friends embarked on one last canoe trip before the biting cold. Little did they know this journey would soon become a fight for survival against the unexpected forces of nature.

As they paddled their way across the river, relishing in the beauty of the changing leaves, a sudden storm erupted, catching the group off guard. The once calm waters became a tumultuous sea, violently rocking their canoe. In the chaos, the churning water threw Stephen out, instantly separating him from his friends and the safety of the boat.

As Stephen desperately fought against the merciless current, he struggled to keep his head above water. In those harrowing moments, his life seemed to flash before his eyes for the third time. His mind raced, capturing glimpses of his friends' worried faces, his unfulfilled dreams, and the life he yearned to live.

Just as Stephen's strength waned, and he questioned his ability to hold on any longer, a glimmer of hope appeared. A rope suddenly looped around his body, acting as an unexpected lifeline. Chris, their gentle and introverted member, had tied the rope to the canoe. Astonishingly, he'd thrown it with remarkable accuracy.

United in their unwavering friendship, the group of friends, now filled with renewed determination, pulled Stephen back to safety. Together, they defied the storm's wrath, displaying the strength that lies within deep connections and the willingness to go to great lengths to save a beloved comrade.

As others hoisted Stephen back into the canoe, gasping for air and overwhelmed with gratitude, he realized the immense power of friendship. Faced with adversity, it was Chris's quiet strength and decisive action that had saved Stephen's life. This unforgettable experience would be a lasting reminder of the strong friendship and the importance of cherishing life's moments. The bond between these friends was unbreakable.

A New Outlook: Living Life to the Fullest

In life, we often take the simplest pleasures for granted, only to realize their true significance when faced with mortality. For Stephen, a series of close encounters with death not only heightened his appreciation for life but also deepened the bonds he shared with his friends.

What was once a source of simple joy, the river became a powerful symbol of spirit, courage, and the unbreakable soul that lies within each of us. Stephen's friends' unwavering support taught him that challenges awaken inner strength and stamina, not break us. Stephen's near-death experiences changed his outlook on life. Now he lives each day to the fullest, faces challenges head-on, and values his friendships.

Stephen's first brush with death shook him to the core, making him acutely aware of the fragility and value of life. The near-death experience forced him to reevaluate his priorities and embrace a newfound gratitude for every moment. From simple joys like a warm cup of coffee to the beauty of nature, Stephen savored every experience with renewed enthusiasm.

Once a place of innocent fun, the river took on a deeper meaning for Stephen after his encounters with death. The river became a metaphor for the ebb and flow of life's challenges, highlighting the importance of strength and the ability to adapt.

Standing by the river's edge, Stephen found solace in the rhythmic flow of water, reminding him of the strength within himself and his friends. Stephen acknowledges he owes his life to the unwavering support of his friends, who repeatedly pulled him back from the brink. Through these life-altering experiences, Stephen realized the true value of friendship and the profound impact it can have on one's life. The shared experiences of facing mortality together strengthened their bonds, creating a support system that was unbreakable.

Stephen's journey, filled with brushes with death, taught him invaluable lessons about the flexibility of the human spirit and the transformative power of friendship. Each day, he fully embraced life, knowing that challenges do not break us but awaken our inner strength.

The river, once a simple source of joy, now serves as a constant reminder of the courage and determination that lies within each of us. As Stephen continues to cherish the unwavering support of his friends, he inspires others to face their own challenges with renewed vigor and appreciation for the beauty of life.

Stephen grew with each passing season. He grew in gratitude, bravery, and understanding. He realized life's challenges help discover potential.

8

Mary Ellen's Legacy

———◆◆◆◆———

Mary Ellen lived in the small town of Wilson on the tranquil banks of Lake Rustin. Mary Ellen's life was mostly uneventful. She worked at the local library, surrounded by the musty smell of old books and the soft rustle of pages turning. Although surrounded by people and their stories every day, there was a part of Mary Ellen that felt like her own story was about to be forgotten.

Each day, Mary Ellen would welcome library patrons with a warm smile and help them find the information they sought. She found joy in recommending books to readers and seeing the look of excitement on their faces when they dove into a new world or gained a new perspective. However, while wading through the endless tides of stories and knowledge, Mary Ellen felt invisible.

She had always been a quiet and introverted person who preferred to escape into the world of books. However, as the years went by, she wondered whether she had a story worth telling. Would anyone mention her name after she was long gone? Would she leave a positive imprint on the world?

Mary Ellen wanted more. She wanted adventure, excitement, and a way to make her life stand out from the mundane. She longed to break free from the monotony of her daily routine and leave an impression on the people she met. The library, which was filled with the stories of others, only fueled her desire for something more.

One evening, as Mary Ellen was shelving books in the library, she stumbled upon an old leather-bound journal. Picking it up, she flipped through its pages. Handwritten stories, poems, and sketches from people who had used the journal over the years filled it.

As she read the varied collection of stories, Mary Ellen's heart raced with excitement. This journal was the key to unlocking her own story. With a shaky hand, she made a decision that would change her life. She would become a part of this mysterious journal's history, adding her own stories of triumph, love, and self-discovery.

From that day on, Mary Ellen began writing in the journal for every experience.

Mary Ellen's fear of being forgotten disappeared with time. She realized it wasn't about how many people remembered her name, but about the impact she had on those she met. Mary Ellen's adventures and storytelling inspired others. They encouraged them to live their own lives and create their own experiences.

Mary Ellen has always been a traveler, going on thrilling expeditions to the remotest parts of the world, immersing herself in diverse cultures, and taking in the landscapes. She has climbed the highest peaks of the Himalayas and dived to the deepest parts of the Great Barrier Reef, all while following her passion for exploration. Along the way, she meets people and, through her curiosity and an open mind, forms connections with them.

Mary Ellen's gift for storytelling is unparalleled. Every story she tells transports her listeners to another time and place, painting vivid pictures with her words. Her captivating stories of majestic African elephants and the ethereal Northern Lights enthralled her audiences.

However, it was not just the amazing stories and adventures that made the people remember. Mary Ellen was an enthusiastic person, and her passion was infectious. She loved exploring the unknown and having new experiences, and it inspired other people to step out of their comfort zones and look for their own adventures. She believed everyone should live life to the fullest, and she told everyone she met that.

Through her interactions and the stories she told, Mary Ellen inspired people to find beauty and potential in their own lives. She told them every day was a chance to grow, find yourself, and make memories. She believed that every action, gesture, and encounter could have a positive effect on individuals and the world.

Mary Ellen's journey has become much more than just a personal quest for adventure; it has become a mission to inspire and encourage others to live their lives with purpose and passion. It is not the number of people who will remember her legacy that matters, but the positive influence she has left behind. Mary Ellen's story shows that even small actions can make a difference. Our lives impact those around us.

In the end, the journal held many tales, and Mary Ellen's story was part of it, a tapestry of human experience future generations would cherish. She realized her life was not ordinary and that by using the power of storytelling, she had found her own unique voice in the world.

Mary Ellen eventually settled in a small village called Green Hollow, which was home to a close-knit and vibrant community of people. Mary Ellen spent her time at the local community center, helping to plan events and support the elderly. She made friends easily.

In Green Hollow, Mary Ellen met an aged woman named Margaret. Margaret had spent her entire life in the village and knew all the stories. She told Mary Ellen about the history of the village, its people, their triumphs and tragedies, and the importance of the community. Margaret became a guide to Mary Ellen, teaching her the value of connections and the power of storytelling.

Inspired by Margaret, Mary Ellen put the stories of Green Hollow into a book. She spent her days talking to the residents, recording their memories, and weaving them into a tapestry of words. As she listened to their stories, Mary Ellen realized everyone had a fear of being forgotten, but it was their connections with others that kept their memories alive.

Mary Ellen's book took months to finish. The villagers anxiously awaited its completion and the printed stories of their lives and Green Hollow's history. Mary Ellen had found a sense of purpose and fulfillment that she had never known before.

One evening, Mary Ellen sat with Margaret and watched the sunset over the village. Mary Ellen was no longer afraid of being forgotten. She had found a place and people who would remember her. The book she was creating was not just a collection of stories; it was a testament to the power of human connection.

Readers gave Mary Ellen's book, *The Heart of Green Hollow*, a warm reception upon publication. It became a precious part of the village's heritage, a reminder of the importance of community and personal impact. Mary Ellen continued her journey, traveling from village to village, sharing related stories, and leaving her mark on the world.

In the end, it was not the book that ensured Mary Ellen's remembrance; it was the lives she touched, the connections she made, and the love she shared. She learned that to be remembered, one does not have to do something great or extraordinary; it is the impact that one has on the surrounding people.

And so, Mary Ellen's journey continues: a journey of love, connection, and the timeless power of storytelling. Mary Ellen was free from her fear of being forgotten and replaced with a legacy of memories that would live on in the hearts of those she touched and would never forget her.

9

Eli and the Circle of Life

In the land of Ancient Israel, the terrain comprised fertile plains and towering hills. At Shiloh, behind the hills, you could see the sunset casting a golden hue on the tabernacle, which was at the heart of Israel's spiritual life. Here, Eli, the venerable high priest, dedicated his life to serving God.

His wisdom was legendary, his faith unwavering. A man of quiet strength, his lined face spoke years of devotion, of sacrifice. His white beard flowed like a river of wisdom, his eyes, though aged, still holding a spark of divine inspiration. He wore the sacred vestments of the high priest with dignity, the breastplate of judgment gleaming with twelve precious stones, each representing one of the twelve tribes of Israel.

The tabernacle itself was a marvel, a portable sanctuary that was the focal point of worship and sacrifice. Inside its walls, God was palpable, the Ark of the Covenant, inside the Most Holy Place, behind the veil, adorned with golden cherubim.

To maintain the sacred space, to conduct religious rituals, Eli, the high priest, served. He spent his days offering prayers and sacrifices for the people, seeking divine guidance, and providing spiritual counsel. The tabernacle was both physical structure and symbol of God's covenant with the Israelites, representing their unique bond and status as His chosen people. Through Eli's dedicated service, the people of Israel found solace, guidance, and a deep connection to their faith.

But Eli carried a heavy burden, one that wouldn't leave him alone. His sons, Hophni and Phinehas, were a constant source of anguish to him. Their actions, corrupt and sinful, were exactly the opposite of what Eli himself wished to see. The people whispered of their misdeeds, and Eli's heart ached, knowing he had failed to guide them.

This dramatic change in the spiritual life of Eli and the Israelites began with a divine vision one night. A radiant light filled the room, illuminating every corner with its ethereal glow. Trembling with awe, Eli heard a voice calling his name. It was a voice unlike any he had ever heard — powerful, yet gentle; commanding, yet comforting. In that moment, Eli knew without a doubt that God was summoning him.

This divine vision would forever change the course of Eli's life. It solidified his calling to serve as a high priest, a role he would embrace with fervent devotion. From that night forward, Eli dedicated himself wholeheartedly to the service of God and the people. He would become known for his wisdom, compassion, and his unwavering commitment to upholding the sacred traditions of his faith.

Eli, as a high priest, faced many challenges and obstacles as he embarked on his journey. However, his unwavering faith and deep connection to the divine guided him through every trial. Eli would make significant contributions to the religious community; he would lead with humility, compassion, and an unwavering commitment to God's word. His story would inspire generations to come, serving as a testament to the power of faith and the transformative impact of a divine calling.

As the high priest of Shiloh, Eli performed sacred duties daily. He supervised the sacrificial offerings, making sure they met divine law. His aged hands moved steadily as he performed the rituals that connected the people to their Creator. Eli's devotion to his role as high priest brought a sense of peace and reverence to the tabernacle, where his presence was deeply respected. His wisdom and deep understanding of spiritual matters guided the Israelites in their pursuit of a meaningful relationship with God.

Eli, however, influenced the tabernacle and the people who came to it. People of all levels of society sought his unwavering commitment to righteousness, from commoners in search of solace to chieftains struggling with weighty decisions. Eli was renowned for his wisdom and moral guidance; many regarded him as a source of divine inspiration, seeking his guidance not only in matters of faith but also in matters of personal and communal importance.

Yet, despite his esteemed position and the respect he commanded, Eli faced an ever-growing challenge that threatened to undo all he had worked for. His sons, Hophni and Phinehas, who were also priests, engaged in misconduct that not only tarnished their own reputations but also cast a shadow over the entire priesthood. Their actions, which included exploiting their positions for personal gain and engaging in immoral behavior, were a source of great distress for Eli. He knew that their misconduct not only violated divine law but also undermined the trust and faith of the Israelites in their religious leaders.

Eli, torn between his love for his sons and his commitment to upholding the sanctity of his role, had a tough decision to make. He needed to address the misconduct and restore the spiritual integrity of the priesthood without alienating his own flesh and blood. This would test Eli's leadership and resilience; he faced a crisis that could split his community, requiring him to balance justice and family loyalty.

Hophni and Phinehas, Eli's sons, were a source of great sorrow. Their actions were a stark contrast to their father's teachings. They exploited their positions, taking the best portions of the sacrifices for themselves and engaging in immoral behavior with the women who served at the entrance of the tabernacle. Their actions dishonored their family and desecrated their sacred duties.

Eli's heart ached with grief. He loved his sons dearly, yet he knew their actions were an affront to God. His attempts to correct them had been fruitless, and the people had lost faith in him. The internal struggle was palpable as he grappled with his responsibilities as both a father and a high priest.

One day, Samuel, a prophet, delivered a divine message to Eli one day. The message was serious. God chose Samuel to be a prophet, and he delivered the divine warning to Eli. God had seen the corruption within his household, particularly the wickedness of his sons, Hophni and Phinehas, who were priests themselves. The consequences were dire — Eli's lineage would suffer, and his sons would face divine retribution.

The warning weighed heavily on Eli, as he realized the gravity of the situation. Yet, despite the turmoil and the impending judgment, Eli continued to serve God with unwavering devotion. He understood that his responsibility as a high priest was to uphold the spiritual well-being of the people, even if it meant facing personal tragedy.

Eli sought solace in prayer, spending countless hours in the tabernacle, asking for God's mercy and guidance. He witnessed the consequences of his sons' actions, testing his resolve, yet his belief in divine justice never wavered. His unyielding commitment overshadowed Eli's moments of doubt to his spiritual duties, as he remained faithful to God.

In the tabernacle's quiet, Eli, a devout and righteous priest, often found solace in deep reflection on his life and the failings that weighed heavily on his heart. He earnestly sought forgiveness, not only for his own transgressions but also for the shortcomings of his sons, who had strayed from the path of righteousness. Eli's repentance was genuine, his heart laid bare before God as he humbly pleaded for mercy and restoration. Through the trials and tribulations that tested his faith, Eli's devotion to God only grew stronger, shining like a beacon of hope amidst the darkness that surrounded him.

The fateful day finally arrived when the Israelites, under the leadership of Eli, were to confront their arch-rivals, the Philistines, in a decisive battle. The air crackled with tension as the two formidable armies clashed on the battlefield, each desperate to secure a victory that would shape their destiny.

Desperate and believing in divine power, the Israelites moved the Ark of the Covenant to the front lines, hoping for a miracle. The Israelites placed their faith in the Ark, trusting that it would serve as a conduit for God's intervention and deliverance.

However, unbeknownst to them, they had misplaced their faith. The Philistines, driven by their own fierce determination and military prowess, gained the upper hand in the battle, overpowering the Israelites with their superior strategy and strength. The superior Philistines inflicted bitter disappointment and a devastating defeat on the once-hopeful Israelites. This turn of events left them questioning the very foundation of their beliefs and the role of the sacred Ark in their lives.

Thus, the story of Eli and the Israelites serves as a powerful reminder of the complexities of faith and the consequences of misplaced trust. It is a tale of humility, repentance, and the enduring struggle to find redemption in the face of adversity. Eli's unwavering devotion and his sincere desire for forgiveness continue to inspire believers to reflect and seek spiritual growth, even in times of despair and uncertainty.

In the chaos of battle, the sons of Eli fell. Their tragic demise marked the fulfillment of the prophecy that foretold their doom. As the dust settled, their enemies had captured the Israelites, and the devastating reality set in.

Word of this immense loss reached Eli, the high priest and father of the fallen brothers. Overwhelmed by grief, Eli could not bear the weight of the tragedy that had befallen his family and his people. Consumed by despair, he stumbled and fell from his seat, his neck snapping upon impact. In that moment, Eli's life came to a tragic end, leaving the Israelites even more desolate and in mourning. Losing their sons and the sacred Ark marked a dark chapter in their history, a chapter they would forever remember.

Eli faced a tragic demise that marked the end of a significant era. As high priest and judge of Israel, Eli lived a life filled with spiritual experiences and profound moral dilemmas. His story powerfully illustrates the complexities of faith and the dire results of neglecting one's duty to God. Eli's failure to discipline his sons, who indulged in corrupt practices, led to their deaths and the downfall of his own lineage.

Despite the tragedy, Eli's legacy persisted and continued to influence future generations. His story served as a cautionary tale, a constant reminder of the vital importance of spiritual integrity and the dire consequences of ignoring moral decay. The lessons learned from Eli's mistakes became a guiding light for those who sought to lead Israel along the righteous path.

As for Eli, he left behind a vacuum in leadership that needed to be filled. It was then that the Israelites anointed a new leader to guide them during these challenging times. The choice was simple yet crucial; they chose Samuel, that young prophet whom God had called to be a leader to the nation.

Under Samuel's guidance, Israel experienced a revival of faith and renewed strength. The people found solace and inspiration in Samuel's teachings, as he tirelessly sought to restore their connection with God. With his prophetic visions and wise counsel, Samuel led the nation towards a path of spiritual growth and moral rectitude.

The circle of life continued, and Eli's legacy continued to shape the destiny of Israel. The lessons learned from his story echoed through the generations, reminding people of the importance of faith, discipline, and moral responsibility. Eli's tragic end marked a turning point. However, his impact continues to be felt by those inspired by his life.

10

The Journey of Forgiveness

ast mistakes and grievances haunted Charlotte, a successful but emotionally scarred professional. The weight of her previous missteps,
the pain she had caused others, the opportunities she had let slip away, all
hung around her neck, unforgiven. Her past scars left her feeling isolated
and disconnected from people, even though, on the surface, Charlotte had
her life together. Instead of inner peace, she yearned for a release from the
burdens that held her back.

One day, Charlotte stumbled upon a flyer for a workshop on forgiveness
led by Dr. Martin, a renowned therapist and healer. Intrigued and desperate for a change, Charlotte signed up for the workshop without knowing
that it would be the beginning of a journey of self-discovery, healing, and
transformation.

When Charlotte arrived at the workshop, a diverse group of people
greeted her, all there to find comfort and relief from past hurt. Dr. Martin created a safe space for vulnerability and growth. He led participants
through exercises, discussions, and sessions focused on forgiveness, empathy, and self-acceptance.

Alongside the other workshop attendees, Charlotte confronted her past
mistakes and grievances and, finally, unraveled the layers of pain that
had imprisoned her for so long. Through open and honest dialogue, she

learned that forgiveness is not about condoning or forgetting but about freeing oneself from the chains of resentment and bitterness.

Over the days, a serious transformation occurred that changed her life. She learned to let go of her past, to embrace her imperfections, and to seize the power of forgiveness. Every session left her heart feeling a little lighter as she rebuilt the bridges she once burned. With the support and understanding of her fellow participants, Charlotte found solace and a new sense of belonging.

At the end of the forgiveness workshop, Charlotte emerged as a new woman. The heavy burden of her past mistakes and grievances was gone. Instead, she walked away with a renewed sense of purpose, inner peace, and the tools she needed to manage future challenges with grace and forgiveness. The effect of forgiveness in one's life is powerful, as Charlotte's journey shows.

The power of forgiveness! To forgive is to set ourselves free from anger, to stop resenting, to heal the emotional wounds, and to restore peace within us. It is the conscious decision to put an end to the negative emotions that have eaten us up inside. By forgiving people, we can leave behind the burdens of the past and move forward with a clearer, kinder, and more compassionate mind. It is a powerful act of love and growth that helps people develop better relationships with other people and with themselves.

Forgiveness can fix broken relationships, join the gaps that were once there, and create peace through reconciliation to make the world a more harmonious and understanding place. It is the recognition that we are all humans, we all make mistakes, and that by extending forgiveness, we create an environment of empathy, understanding, and healing.

The effect of forgiveness is amazing. It can restore hope, heal the heart, and bring about a profound personal and collective transformation.

I saw a friendship end in a conflict based on a misunderstanding when I was a kid. It all began when my friend and I disagreed on a minor issue. Instead of talking it through, we engaged in a war of words and said some things that were hurtful. The consequences of that were dire; they permanently damaged the friendship that once existed between the two of us. There was a layer of unspoken regret between us, and not one of us made the first move to fix our friendship.

As the days turned into weeks and the weeks into months, I thought a lot about what our friendship meant to me. The time we had spent together, the jokes we had shared, and the support that we had given one another all came flooding back into my mind. I knew that losing such a friend over a misunderstanding was something I couldn't bear.

Wanting to repair our broken friendship, I contacted my friend and offered an olive branch. We both need to heal. It was a nerve-wracking moment not knowing how my friend would react. Although doubts initially lingered, the life-changing and remarkable power of forgiveness became strikingly clear. My friend and I surprised and relieved me by accepting my reconciliation attempt.

We got together and had a real talk, and we both said what was mistaken and apologized for our parts in it. That is when I saw the radical nature of forgiveness in action. It can restore hope, heal the heart, and bring about significant personal and collective growth.

We both felt a weight lift off our shoulders as we forgave each other and found this new sense of freedom. Our friendship was reborn, but it was stronger and more resilient than before. We became more open, understanding, and diligent in our relationship.

This experience taught me a valuable lesson: Holding grudges only makes the heart bitter and the mind resentful, while forgiveness clears the way for growth and a brighter future. My friend and I are still friends today, and we cherish the lessons we learned on our forgiveness journey.

We know we will have conflicts again, but we are prepared to deal with them better with the knowledge and understanding we have gained. Forgiveness not only restored our friendship, but it was beneficial; it also transformed us as individuals.

In conclusion, the act of forgiving—and being forgiven—renewed our friendship. It taught me the importance of humility, empathy, and the ability to let go of past grievances. Through forgiveness, we appreciate our friendship even more than before. It has become a testament to the strength and resilience of our bond, showing that it is worth fighting for.

We each need our own transformative healing workshop. It could help us tremendously.

However, it is important to note that while forgiveness can be beneficial, it is not always easy or necessary. Some situations may warrant confrontation and resolution rather than forgiveness. One can forgive someone without reconciling with them; therefore, do not confuse forgiveness with reconciliation. Forgiveness is a choice that can have positive consequences for both the forgiver and the forgiven.

11

Grandma's Cameo

———◆◆◆———

It was a soft, peaceful place. Memories danced in the warm glow of the afternoon light, a sanctuary within the hushed whispers of caregivers and the gentle hum of activity. From behind the lace curtains, the sun's rays filtered through the nursing home room, casting patterns on the walls of the cozy room.

Eleanor sat in her favorite armchair, her wrinkled hands gently cradling a small velvet box, wrapped in a reverence that spoke of its significance. Her eyes, now dimmed by time, still sparkled with the wisdom and experience of a lifetime.

Eleanor opened the box with a reverence that spoke of its significance. There was an exquisite piece of jewelry, a cameo, handed down through generations. The ivory profile of a graceful woman is under her touch, enclosed in delicate gold filigree, as if it were coming alive. Her great-grandmother gave the cameo to Eleanor on the eve of her marriage, and Eleanor carried it through seventy years and many life chapters.

As she held the cameo, memories flooded her mind. That day, she received it with excitement and nervous anticipation. Her great-grandmother, a woman of few words but boundless wisdom, had placed the cameo in her hands with a tender smile. "Take care of this, Eleanor," she had said. "Our family has owned this for generations. It carries the strength and resilience of the women who came before you. It will be both your guide and your guardian."

Eleanor's heart swelled with pride and responsibility as she accepted the precious gift. She was completely unaware that the cameo would unexpectedly involve her in its unfolding events.

The cameo had witnessed the joy of her wedding day and the sparkle of her eyes as she exchanged vows with her beloved Henry. It had been there through the early years of their marriage, as they built a home filled with love and laughter. It had felt the gentle caress of her fingers as she soothed her children to sleep, a symbol of continuity and tradition.

But life, with all its beauty and unpredictability, also brought challenges. The cameo had been a silent witness to moments of heartache and sorrow. Clasped it in her hand when she received the news of Henry's passing, finding it a steady anchor in a sea of grief. Throughout all of that, the cameo remained a constant link to the strength and resilience of her ancestors.

Her son, John, tragically lost his life while serving in Afghanistan. He was a brave and dedicated soldier who had made the ultimate sacrifice for his country. Unimaginable for Eleanor, but she found solace in the memories they shared and the knowledge that he had fought for a cause he believed in.

Besides that, she had also experienced the devastating loss of her daughter, Emily, several years prior. A tragic car wreck cut short Emily's life, leaving Eleanor heartbroken and feeling as if her world had shattered into a million pieces.

The void left by both her children was unbearable, and Eleanor often longed for their presence. As Eleanor reflected on her life, she couldn't help but wonder about the future of a precious family heirloom—a beautifully crafted cameo generations had passed down. It held immense sentimental value and had become a symbol of the strength and tenacity of her family.

However, with the passing of her children and no grandchildren to pass it on to, Eleanor pondered whether this would mark the end of the cameo's extraordinary journey. The cameo has witnessed the joys and sorrows of Eleanor's ancestors, surviving countless trials and tribulations. Generations have cherished and treasured the cameo, serving as a tangible connection to the past. Eleanor couldn't bear the thought of its story ending abruptly, without a worthy recipient to carry on with its legacy.

With a heavy heart, Eleanor contemplated the idea of finding someone deserving of inheriting the cameo. She yearned for someone who would appreciate its significance and keep the spirit of her family alive. There was perhaps a distant relative or a close friend who would embrace the cameo's history and carry it forward into the future.

As Eleanor grappled with these thoughts, she realized that the cameo's journey was not yet over. It had withstood the test of time, and she was determined to ensure that its story would continue. Eleanor resolved to search for a worthy custodian, someone who would honor and cherish the cameo as much as her family.

Little did she know that fate had a way of intervening, and the next chapter in the cameo's journey was about to unfold. The cameo has accompanied Eleanor throughout the years, even into the nursing home. There, new friendships have developed, and she has shared memories of the past as if they were precious treasures.

One day, as Eleanor sat by the window, her young nurse Sarah approached her. The cameo and the stories Eleanor shared about its journey had always intrigued Sarah. "Eleanor, would you mind telling me more about the cameo?" Sarah asked, her eyes filled with genuine curiosity.

Eleanor smiled warmly, grateful for the opportunity to share the tale once more. "This cameo has been in my family for generations," she began. "My great-grandmother on the eve of my wedding gave it to me. She told me it carried the strength of the women who came before me. And oh, the places it has been!"

Eleanor's voice wove a tapestry of memories, recounting the joys and sorrows, the love and loss that had marked her life. Sarah listened intently, captivated by the rich history encapsulated in the small piece of jewelry.

As Eleanor spoke, she realized the cameo was not just a symbol of her past but a bridge to the future. It carried within it the stories of generations, a legacy that would live on long after she was gone.

"Sarah," Eleanor said softly, "I want you to have the cameo." Sarah's eyes widened in surprise.

"Eleanor, I couldn't possibly—"

Eleanor insisted, "You must." "You're like a granddaughter to me. You've shown me so much kindness and care. This cameo carries the strength and resilience of the women who came before us. I want you to carry it forward."

With trembling hands, Eleanor placed the cameo in Sarah's palm. It was a moment of profound significance, a passing of the torch from one generation to the next.

Tears welled in Sarah's eyes as she accepted the precious gift. "Thank you, Eleanor. I'll cherish it always."

As the sun cast a golden glow over the nursing home's courtyard, Eleanor felt at peace in her rocking chair. The day's weariness lifted from her soul. She felt that her responsibilities with the Cameo were over. She had given it to Sarah with one condition: she was to retell its story to her children and her grandchildren, keeping the story alive.

Sarah had promised to do that, and Eleanor was most pleased. The cameo, alongside its stories, could bring joy and inspiration to those who owned it and listened to its history. It could transport people to another time and place, connecting them to the struggles and triumphs of their ancestors. The stories of the cameo were not bound by time; they served as reminders of love's power, stamina, and our enduring connections.

Eleanor's vision for the cameo's legacy was clear. It would, she ensured, remain a source of strength and inspiration for generations. She feverishly drafted the stories and memories associated with the cameo that afternoon, meticulously preserving each detail in a beautiful note for Sarah. The cameo's legacy extended beyond mere jewelry; it symbolized enduring love, strength, and timeless bonds. It became a beacon of hope, reminding humanity that despite the passing of years and the trials we face, we are all part of a larger narrative.

Eleanor, with her unwavering dedication and love for the cameo, had ensured that its message would continue to inspire and unite people for generations to come.

That Tuesday morning, Sarah made her way down the hall to Eleanor's room and found the room empty. The nursing home staff told her that Eleanor, her beloved friend, had passed peacefully the evening before.

On her bedside table, surrounded by photos and trinkets, was a card for Sarah. It read, "Sarah, my dear, you are the future generation I have prayed for. The cameo I gave you yesterday will remind you of its power and your own strength. When you hold it, remember me. When you share it with your children or grandchildren, remind them of the stories I have shared with you. God bless you, Sarah. Love, Eleanor."

In Sarah's heart, the words of Eleanor resonated deeply, a mix of sadness and gratitude. Her friend, Eleanor, was gone, but this sentimental gift made her absence even more significant. Generations passed down the cameo, a beautifully crafted piece of jewelry with delicate carvings, symbolizing their family's strength and endurance.

As Sarah traced her fingers over the intricate details, she could almost feel Eleanor's presence, as though she were guiding her from beyond. This simple object became a tangible connection to her dear friend's wisdom, love, and the countless stories she had shared throughout the past few weeks.

The cameo will serve as a treasured heirloom, carrying the memories of Eleanor, family stories, and the lessons of generations. It would become a source of strength, reminding Sarah of the abilities that lived within her and inspiring her to overcome any challenges that life might present.

With a heavy heart, Sarah carefully tucked the card and cameo into her bag, vowing to honor her friend's legacy by carrying her stories forward. As she left the empty room, a profound sense of gratitude washed over her.

While Eleanor may no longer be physically present, her love, guidance, and wisdom would forever remain imprinted upon Sarah's heart, ready to be shared with future generations. The cameo lives on!

12

It Reminds Me of Home

❖

There was something about the smell of Mama's hot biscuits that made the world feel safe. Her biscuits were golden; the soft insides of the biscuits melted in your mouth, especially when there was homemade strawberry jam on top of them. Each bite offered the comforting warmth of a kitchen hug. Her pecan pies, I remember, were no less vivid in my mind. I remember sitting at the wooden table, the aroma of sweet syrup and roasted pecans in the air. The first bite was always the best—the crunch of the pecans, the sweet, gooey filling, and the buttery crust that crumbled just so. Our small-town people made a buzz about Mama's pies every Thanksgiving, asking if she had made one.

Mama's hot biscuits were our household staple, a delicious treat that made our mornings comfortable and joyful. Just the sight of them, steaming fresh from the oven, was enough to make anyone's mouth water. The outside was a golden crust, slightly crispy, and the inside was fluffy and tender, almost melting in your mouth. Mama's homemade strawberry jam made the biscuits exceptional. The jam, from backyard strawberries, added a burst of sweetness that perfectly complemented the biscuits' buttery, savory flavor.

It wasn't just the taste that made Mama's hot biscuits special, though. It was the love and care she put into making them. I can still picture her in the kitchen, her hands flour dusted as she kneaded the dough, her apron tied tightly around her waist. The warm, inviting scent of freshly baked biscuits filled the entire house and drew everyone in like a magnet.

Just like her biscuits, Mama's pecan pies were a work of art. She would spend hours on end preparing the filling, toasting the pecans to bring out their rich, nutty flavor. The result was a pie that was a symphony of textures and flavors. The crunch of the pecans was a beautiful contrast to the sweet, gooey filling, and the buttery crust was the perfect vessel for this delectable creation.

Word of Mama's pecan pies spread like wildfire throughout our town. Every Thanksgiving, people would eagerly await Mama's pies, hoping to get a slice of this heavenly dessert. It became a tradition for our family to share these pies with our neighbors and friends, a gesture of love and gratitude during the holiday season.

Mama's hot biscuits and pecan pies were more than just food; they were a symbol of love, comfort, and togetherness. As the sun peered through the kitchen window in the morning, Mama would roll out the dough with her gentle hands, infusing it with her unwavering affection. The oven baked the biscuits, filling the air with a tantalizing aroma that lured us all to the table. We'd all gather around, waiting for Mama to put the golden-brown biscuits on a platter, and we'd feel the warmth seep through our fingertips as we reached for one. With every fluffy bite, we could taste the love Mama had kneaded into each batch.

And then there were the pecan pies, a true masterpiece that Mama crafted with precision and care. She would put the pecans on the crust with such precision that every slice would have the perfect amount of nutty goodness. The sweet scent of caramelized sugar filled the house as the pie baked to a golden perfection, enticing us to sneak a peek into the oven with anticipation. When the time was right, Mama would take the pie out of the oven, and its surface would glisten in the warm kitchen light.

These cherished treats were more than just culinary delights; they represented the heart and soul of our home. The simple act of breaking bread together became a cherished tradition when we could put aside our worries, savor the comfort, and love each other.

Mama's kitchen was a haven, a place where laughter and stories flowed freely and where we felt safe and loved. The memories of those moments linger on, forever etched in our minds and hearts. Even to this day, the smell of biscuits or a pecan pie transports me back to Mama's kitchen instantly. Her love and warmth were in every bite.

These days, those scents and tastes are just memories, but they're powerful ones. After Mama passed, I found her old recipe book, worn and stained from years of use. It was a treasure trove of culinary secrets, filled with handwritten notes and splatters of ingredients.

With a mix of nostalgia and determination, I embarked on a journey to recreate the flavors of my childhood. I carefully followed Mama's recipes, measuring each ingredient with precision and paying attention to every detail. The first batch of biscuits came out of the oven disappointingly dry, lacking the moist and fluffy texture I remembered.

I didn't stop there; I adjusted the recipe, experimenting with different ratios of flour and butter. It took a few more tries, but I could finally get the perfect balance and have biscuits that are tender and melt-in-your-mouth delicious.

The next challenge was the pie filling. Mama's pies always delightfully combined sweet and tangy, but my initial attempts resulted in fillings that were too runny and caused the crust to become soggy. Still, I didn't give up; I adjusted the amount of thickening agent and added a touch of more salt to balance the sweetness.

Each attempt brought me closer to recreating the exact taste and consistency that Mama effortlessly achieved. Recreating Mama's recipes was a labor of love, a journey of trial and error that honored her memory and kept her alive in my kitchen.

When I bake, it's like a conversation with Mama. I can almost hear her voice guiding me, laughing at my mistakes, and cheering me on when I get it right. The kitchen fills with those familiar smells, and for a moment, she's there with me again. It's in those moments that I realize home isn't just a place—it's a feeling, a collection of memories tied to the senses.

When I sit at that same wooden table and enjoy a slice of pecan pie, I know Mama would be proud. She'd smile that warm smile of hers and say, "It reminds me of home."

That table, weathered and worn from years of family gatherings and shared meals, holds a special place in my heart. It has witnessed countless conversations, laughter, and tears that are now a part of our family's history.

Mama, with her culinary expertise, would often fill the air with the sweet aroma of freshly baked pies, just like the one I'm savoring now. The pecan pie, with its perfectly caramelized nuts and buttery crust, brings back memories of Mama's kitchen and the love and care she poured into every dish. It was more than just a pie; it was a taste of home, a comforting reminder of the warmth and love that filled our house.

Mama's radiant smile, full of pride, would light up the room whenever she saw her family enjoying her homemade creations. She worked tirelessly to recreate the flavors of her childhood, and this table became the gathering place where we celebrated those cherished traditions.

This pecan pie is a taste of Mama's legacy. It's filled with her love, and I feel her presence. This table, with its worn edges and faded memories, holds the essence of our family, and I am grateful for the moments we shared around it.

13

The Weight of Memories

❖

In the charming southern town of Statesboro, Georgia, a man named Brian Adams lived. This was a place where, as you drove through the picturesque landscape with its sprawling oak trees that whispered to the wind, Brian had lived for as long as he could remember.

Statesboro was both nostalgic and modern, its streets lined with quaint shops and cafes, along with state-of-the-art facilities and bustling business districts. But time had stood still for Brian. Every street corner he passed, every worn brick building he admired, every rustling of the leaves under the wind brought back a flood of memories that he couldn't just wipe away.

Every corner held a story, every building held a part of his past, and the rustling of the leaves carried the whispers of lost conversations and laughter. Statesboro was not just a town to Brian, it was a tapestry of his memories and experiences, embedded into the very fabric of his being.

Now, Brian is just a retired history professor, a man who inspired countless students with his knowledge and passion. His deep voice was legendary, such that he could make even the dullest of historical facts sound like the most compelling tales. However, three years ago, his wife, Eleanor, passed away, and since then, Brian has found it hard to move on. He found solace in the old house they lived in, a charming Victorian with creaking floorboards that echoed with their shared memories.

The once meticulously maintained garden has long since overgrown, a consequence of Eleanor's absence. Brian spent most of his days surrounded by things that reminded him of Eleanor; her spirit was present in every corner of the house.

Eleanor was an exceptionally talented artist. Her paintings were famous for their vibrant colors and raw emotions, her work adorning galleries and homes and captivating viewers with its beauty and depth. She had a rare ability to capture the essence of life and transform the mundane into the extraordinary. Every brush stroke brought her canvases to life, telling stories and evoking powerful emotions.

To Brian, her art held a very personal significance; it was a testament of the love they once shared, a love that is now out of his hands. Staring at the paintings that adorn the walls of his home, he can't help but feel haunted by her presence. Every stroke of Eleanor's brush is a painful reminder of a life he can no longer touch, of a love that is now just a memory. What was once vibrant seems muted and dull, just like the emptiness he feels.

Her art, once a source of joy, is always a reminder of Eleanor. He longs for the warmth and beauty of her paintings again. Brian's routine had become his own prison. Every morning, he would wake up at 6:30 a.m., the sound of his alarm clock jolting him out of his sleep. He would stumble into the kitchen, bleary-eyed and craving normalcy. He would measure out his coffee with such precision that he could almost smell the aroma of the perfect brew. With a bit of a shake, he would pour the steaming liquid into his favorite mug, the one Eleanor had given him on their anniversary years ago.

Sitting at the kitchen table, now worn wooden, Brian longingly gazes at the empty chair on the other side. It was Eleanor's spot, where they would share their hopes and dreams, their breakfasts. Now it's just a constant reminder of her absence, a void that seems impossible to fill.

The soft crackling of the vinyl records on the turntable is the only sound in the room. The old records he has curated over the years contain a symphony of memories within them. As the needle glides across the grooves of the discs, each song is a painful reminder of the dances they used to share, the laughter they used to share in each other's arms. The melodies fill the air, a bittersweet embrace that brings emotions Brian both wishes to forget and is reluctant to let go of.

The scent of Eleanor's perfume, a delicate mix of jasmine and vanilla, is still in the air, as if she had just left. A ghostly presence, her past presence and her enduring memory intertwined with Brian's morning routine, won't leave. The scent is both comforting and torturous to him; it reminds him of the love they shared and the emptiness he felt without her.

In this routine, Brian found both solace and torment. Stability in his upended world came from familiar rituals, yet he wondered if his grief trapped him there, preventing him from moving forward or letting go of the past. The coffee, the empty chair, the records, and the lingering perfume are the bars of his prison, keeping him locked in a cycle of longing and reminiscence for years.

One crisp fall morning, Brian stood in front of the attic door. He hadn't been up there since Eleanor passed away; he didn't want to face the memories that hid in the dusty boxes and forgotten corners of the attic. But something inside him whispered it was time to confront the past, to face the ghosts that had kept him imprisoned.

With a deep breath, he opened the door and climbed the narrow staircase. The attic was a labyrinth of memories, packed with old photo albums, letters, and long-forgotten treasures.

Among the boxes, he found a journal — Eleanor's journal — its leather cover worn and fragile. Eleanor's journal contained her thoughts, sketches, dreams, and fears. On an old, weathered trunk that Brian had inherited from his grandmother, he sat down. That trunk was a treasure trove of memories and emotions, worn, faded wood, and rusty hinges.

As he opened Eleanor's diary, he relived the good and the bad of their time together, the love they shared, and the challenges they faced as a couple. Each page of the diary was a window into Eleanor's soul, her handwritten words a poignant and powerful testimonial to the depth of their connection and the profound pain she had endured.

In her private reflections, she had written about her fear of death, her terror of leaving Brian behind in this world. Yet, even in her own anguish, Eleanor had expressed a heartfelt hope that he would find solace and happiness after she was gone.

The last entry in the diary was a heart-wrenching letter to Brian, a tender farewell brimming with love and unfulfilled yearning. My dearest Brian, she had written. I know that letting go is hard, but you must. You have so much life left to live, so many memories yet to create. I will always be with you in the laughter of our friends, in the world's beauty around you. But you must open your heart to new experiences, to new joys. Let go of the past, my love, and embrace the future.

Tears streamed down Brian's face as he closed the worn leather journal, its pages filled with the heartfelt words of his late wife, Eleanor. Those words she penned with love and vulnerability were like a lifeline, a beacon of hope in the darkness that has consumed him since her passing. For the past few years, grief has relentlessly trapped Brian, unable to let go of the memories and pain that have tied him to the past. But as he read the journal, Eleanor's voice resounded in his heart, reminding him that life was meant to be lived, not merely survived.

In that moment, a glimmer of hope flickered within him, igniting a sense of purpose he had long forgotten. He realized that by clinging to the past, he was not honoring Eleanor's memory; instead, he was imprisoning himself in a world that no longer existed. He silently vowed to embrace the present and future, letting go of his past burden. This, he knew, would best honor Eleanor's memory.

The next morning, Brian woke up with a newfound determination. He had recently inherited his late wife Eleanor's much-beloved garden, a sanctuary that had once been a shared passion. Determined to honor her memory and restore the beauty that had gradually faded over the years, Brian embarked on an arduous journey of reclaiming the garden. With a heavy heart and a sense of purpose, he gathered his tools and set out to breathe new life into the neglected space.

As the sun cast its warm rays upon the earth, Brian immersed himself in the task at hand. He spent hours, and then days, meticulously weeding out the encroaching intruders that had overrun Eleanor's precious plants.

In early spring, he kneeled and carefully planted new seeds, selecting each one to complement the existing flora. With each motion of his hands, he could almost feel Eleanor's presence guiding him through the process. Brian's diligence was unwavering. He spent his time pruning and shaping the overgrown shrubs, coaxing them back to their former glory.

The sound of birdsong filled the air as word of the revitalized garden spread, attracting a symphony of colorful visitors. Butterflies danced from one blossom to another, while bees busied themselves collecting nectar from the vibrant blooms. It was as if Eleanor's spirit had infused the once-dull garden with energy and vitality.

As the days passed, the garden blossomed into a breathtaking tapestry of colors and scents. Unfurling petals revealed their hidden beauty, and the fragrance of blooming flowers filled the gentle breeze. Brian's efforts had not only revived the garden but had also rekindled his own spirit.

Each day, as he tended to the plants, he found solace and a renewed sense of purpose in the garden he had lovingly nurtured back to life. The garden became a sanctuary for Brian, but for all who visited as well. Friends and neighbors, drawn by the captivating allure of the revived space, marveled at the transformation that had taken place. Visitors sensed the love and dedication Brian poured into every aspect of the garden's revival, and Brian's story inspired them.

As Brian stood amidst the blossoming garden, he couldn't help but feel a deep sense of gratitude. Through his unwavering determination, he had not only honored Eleanor's memory but had also created a living testament to their shared love for nature. The garden had become a symbol of resilience and the power of love to breathe new life into the most barren of landscapes.

Brian, gazing at the vibrant tapestry of color and life filling the once-neglected space, knew that he and Eleanor's spirits would always be intertwined with the garden they had nurtured. Brian also reached out to his old friends and colleagues, rekindling relationships that had withered away in his isolation. He started volunteering at the local community center, sharing his knowledge and passion for history with children and adults alike. He even picked up painting again, finding solace in the act of creation, just as Eleanor had done.

As the months turned into years, Brian slowly healed. The weight of the past no longer suffocated him; instead, it became a source of strength and inspiration. He still missed Eleanor every day, but her memory was no longer a burden. It was a gift, a reminder of a love that had shaped his life and would continue to guide him.

One sunny afternoon, as Brian sat in the garden surrounded by the fruits of his labor, he felt a sense of peace that he hadn't known in years. The garden, meticulously planned and nurtured by Brian, was a true testament to his passion for horticulture. Vibrant flowers, lush greenery, bountiful fruits, and vegetables covered every inch of soil. The colors and fragrances intermingled, creating a sensory symphony that brought life and beauty to the air.

As Brian closed his eyes and leaned back in his favorite chair, he could hear the gentle rustling of the leaves in the breeze, swaying in harmony with the soft hum of bees as they moved from bloom to bloom, collecting nectar. And the laughter of children at play served as a joyful reminder of the happiness that nature can bring. In this idyllic moment, Brian found solace and contentment in being able to immerse himself in his garden oasis.

In that moment, Brian understood that letting go didn't mean forgetting. It meant embracing the present, cherishing the memories, and opening your heart to the future. Eleanor would always be a part of him, but he no longer needed to be bound by the past. He was free to live, to love, and to create fresh memories.

As the sun set, casting a warm and radiant golden glow over the garden Brian had so meticulously curated, Brian found himself in a serene atmosphere. The delicate petals of the roses swayed gently in the evening breeze, as if dancing to an ethereal melody. In this moment, a profound sense of gratitude washed over him, and he whispered a silent thank you to Eleanor, his beloved wife. Her presence, though her physical form was gone, remained steadfast in his heart and soul. He knew, with no doubt, that her spirit was still with him, guiding him through life's trials and showering him with unconditional love.

This realization brought indescribable peace to his weary mind, finally allowing him to release the burden he had been carrying. In the fading light of the day, Brian felt a weight lift off his shoulders as he surrendered to the comforting embrace of Eleanor's eternal presence.

14

Unseen Threads

⸎

In the small town of Everwood, in the picturesque countryside of Harper's valley, surrounded by lush greenery, Harry's presence was a beacon of compassion and goodwill. The close-knit community nestled the town in the countryside, and the people always enthusiastically embraced the area's natural beauty and its people.

Harry, a man of humble origins, had left his mark on the town's residents through his kindness and his genuine interest in being a change. Whether it was helping elderly neighbors with their errands or organizing fundraisers for local charities, Harry's generosity knew no bounds.

Although he was struggling financially himself, he never failed to offer help and support to others, always ready to lend a hand or a listening ear to anyone in need. His warm smile and the laughing that could infect caused joy to even the most despondent and unhappy individuals.

The townsfolk admired and respected Harry, not only for his selflessness but also for his unwavering commitment to fostering a sense of community spirit. In Everwood, Harry's presence impacted every corner, from the community center he helped build to the gardens he meticulously tended.

His heart, which was full of compassion, was a treasure trove that was beneficial to all the people he met. Harry's legacy would forever remain etched in the hearts of the townspeople, so they would always remember the power of kindness and what one person can do for a community.

Every morning, without fail, Harry would walk to the town square and whistle a cheerful tune. He owned a little bakery called "Harry's Bakery," famous for its freshly baked bread that had the sunshine inside the crust of the bread. The aroma of his bread alone was enough to draw people from miles away; the mouthwatering scent that filled the air caused them to come.

However, Harry's bakery was more than just a place to buy bread; it was the community's haven. Harry's bakery was a part of the town's social fabric. You would see people gathered outside sipping coffee and chatting while savoring the warm, golden loaves that Harry carefully crafted. The bakery had a cozy interior with a rustic charm and many bread baskets, pastries, and the occasional jar of homemade jam on the shelves. What made Harry's bakery special was that it included the community.

On frigid winter nights, when the wind would howl and send shivers down people's spines, Harry would open his doors to those without shelter. The homeless found solace and warmth inside the bakery, where Harry would offer them a cup of steaming hot coffee and a slice of his fresh bread. At these times, the bakery became a refuge from the harsh realities of life.

Harry's bakery was always at the center of celebrations during festive occasions. Whether it was a joyous wedding or a jubilant holiday, the bakery became the focal point of the celebrations. Harry baked delectable cakes, pastries, and pies, each made with love and attention to detail.

The town's residents would flock to the bakery to fill it with the delight of their laughter, music, and the aroma of freshly baked treats. Beyond his baking skills, Harry had a way of understanding people's needs. He knew when people needed a warm crusty loaf of bread for their day or when they needed a kind word to lift their spirits. Harry's care and compassion were real to everyone who walked through the bakery's door, and he created a sense of belonging.

You could say that Harry's bakery was not just a place to buy bread, but also a place to find comfort, nourishment, and connection. It stood as a proof of how food and kindness can change people's lives and make them more connected than any action of baking.

Life in Everwood seemed to stand still, and Harry thought it would always be that way. But as with all things, change was bound to happen one day.

A large corporation had its eye on the quaint town of Everwood. One spring, their plans unfolded. They planned to build a vast shopping complex that would overshadow Everwood and, more importantly, Harry's bakery. The townsfolk were worried, but Harry remained hopeful. "We've seen tough times before, and we've always come through," he reassured everyone. But deep down, he couldn't shake off the unease gnawing at his heart.

Days turned into weeks, and the construction of the new complex progressed rapidly. Because of the lure of convenience and novelty, the townspeople frequented the new stores. The once busy bakery was now almost empty, and the cheerful tune of Harry had grown faint.

The news spread like wildfire through the tight-knit community and worry gripped the townsfolk. What would become of the cherished traditions and small businesses that were the backbone of Everwood? The threat of change hung over them, casting a dark cloud of uncertainty.

But Harry didn't give up; he remained hopeful and was determined to preserve the spirit of Everwood that he held so dear. He reassured his worried customers, "We've weathered storms before." "We've always adapted and come out stronger. We can't let this new complex define us. Everwood is more than just bricks and mortar; it's the people, the memories, and the love that makes this place special."

Deep down, Harry couldn't shake off the unease gnawing at his heart. He saw the heart and soul of Everwood slipping away, little by little, as the town transformed before his eyes. The sense of community that had once been Everwood's backbone was slowly eroding, replaced by the impersonal allure of consumerism.

As the battle between tradition and progress raged on, Harry found himself at a crossroads. Should he fight to save his bakery, clinging to the hope that the people of Everwood would remember their roots and support local businesses? Or should he accept the inevitable change and find an alternative path, in the very shopping complex that threatened to overshadow his beloved town?

Every day, the fate of Everwood remains unwritten, hanging in the balance. This is a town that was once a welcome refuge to people from the surrounding areas because of its beautiful landscapes, charming cottages, and friendly community. However, as Harry, a lifelong resident of Everwood, contemplates his next move, he wonders whether the relentless march of progress will forever destroy his beloved town's timeless charm. The encroachment of large corporations and their modern developments threatens to transform Everwood into just another faceless suburb, erasing its unique character and sense of community.

Harry knows the decisions made in the coming weeks and months will determine the fate of Everwood, and he feels the weight of that responsibility on his shoulders. The fate of Everwood hangs in the balance. Will he save its beauty and heritage from modernization, or will modernization destroy it forever?

Despite the dwindling customers and the financial challenges, it brought, Harry never wavered in his kindness. He continued to get up every morning, bake bread, and prepare for the day with love and care.

However, as the economic downturn persisted, and more people found themselves unable to afford even the necessities, Harry's bakery faced an increasingly dire situation. The once bustling establishment was now almost empty, with only a few loyal customers coming in occasionally.

Yet Harry's compassion and empathy remained unwavering. Instead of giving up, he took a selfless approach to his predicament. Harry noticed his community members were hungry. He shared his freshly baked bread with them. Despite the financial strain it placed on his struggling business, Harry's priority was to ensure that no one went hungry. His act of kindness not only provided sustenance to those in need but also served as a beacon of hope in a time of uncertainty.

One crisp fall evening, Harry closed the doors of his bakery for what he feared might be the last time. The town square had never felt so still without the sweet aroma of fresh bread filling the air. Harry's heart was heavy, but he forced a smile, knowing he had given his all.

In the days that followed, the townsfolk of Everwood realized that Harry's once vibrant and bustling bakery had vanished. The disappearance of the bakery had abruptly taken away a vital part of their daily lives, leaving an indescribable void. Wandering the streets, the townsfolk missed the familiar smells and friendly greetings of Harry's shop. They noticed new stores had replaced it. These establishments, while undeniably convenient in their offerings, lacked something intangible, something that had made Harry's bakery so special — a warmth, a sense of community.

The townsfolk yearned for the camaraderie that had filled the air as they sipped their morning coffee, exchanged stories, and shared laughter. They missed the genuine conversations that arose from Harry's inviting presence, his ability to know each customer by name, and his genuine interest in their lives. Harry's little shop had been more than just a place to buy bread; it had been the heart and soul of Everwood.

Slowly but surely, the townsfolk understood the true value of what they had lost. One by one, the people of Everwood came together, determined to bring back the heart of their town. They organized fundraisers, spread the word on social media, and even reached out to the press.

The story of Harry's bakery and its impact on the community touched hearts everywhere. On a chilly winter morning, just as the first delicate snowflakes fell, Harry found himself lost in his thoughts. The recent closure of his beloved bakery had left a gap in his heart and a sense of uncertainty about his future.

As he pondered over his next move, a sudden knock on his door startled him from his reverie. Curiosity piqued, Harry cautiously opened the door, only to be met with a heartwarming sight that took his breath away. Standing before him was the entire close-knit community, their faces filled with a glimmer of hope and unwavering support. The townspeople had rallied together, organizing fundraisers, and reaching out to local businesses, determined to help Harry reopen his cherished bakery. The love and generosity that radiated from the crowd was overwhelming, bringing tears of gratitude to Harry's eyes.

With the funds they had raised, Harry's dream of rekindling the warmth and joy of his bakery seemed within reach once again. Together, they had not only raised enough money but also reignited a spark of hope in Harry's heart.

Harry watched the snowflakes dance. He realized this surprise would change his life forever. Harry felt renewed determination and gratitude. Supported by his town and fueled by passion, he was ready to embark on his bakery journey. With tears of gratitude, Harry hugged every one of them.

As he reopened the doors to his beloved bakery, the familiar scent of fresh bread filled the air once more. The townsfolk cheered, knowing they had not only saved a bakery, but had also rekindled the spirit of their community. And as Harry looked around at the smiling faces, he couldn't help but think, "You never know a good thing until it's gone."

15

Life in a Suitcase

Chapter 1: Eviction

Alexandra "Alex" Carter held an eviction notice as she stood in her empty apartment. It was a shocking feeling, losing her job and her home in a week. But Alex refused to let herself become a victim of her circumstances and made the bold decision to leave everything behind and start anew. New Orleans, that city that had always been calling to her in vague whispers, had become her destination of choice.

There was a mix of excitement and trepidation feeling that Alex had as she packed her suitcase. She folded her clothes with attention to detail and picked out the items that she thought would suit the energetic and colorful vibe of her new location. In her toiletries bag, she gathered all the things she would need for her daily routine, knowing that sticking to normal would be important during this time.

Of the two items she was packing, two things held a special place in her heart. The first was a novel written by her late mother and worn and treasured. This book had been with Alex throughout her life, providing comfort and an escape during the tough times. Those pages etched her mother's wisdom, imagination, and invincible spirit, reminding Alex of her inherited strength and spirit.

The second item was a photograph of her childhood home, a cozy little house in some small town. It was a picture of comfort and normalcy that she once knew but was now just a memory. Alex clutched the photograph, knowing that it connected her to her roots and the person she used to be. Leaving her old life behind, she remembered the experiences and lessons that shaped her. These would stay with her in her new apartment.

With her suitcase packed and her heart set, Alex closed the door to her old life and started on the path to a new beginning. The unknown awaited her in the vibrant streets of New Orleans, where she hoped to find not only a fresh start but also a renewed sense of purpose and belonging.

Chapter 2: The Journey

On the train to New Orleans, Alex's anticipation mixed with nervousness as she settled into her seat. Little did she know this train ride would be the start of a life-changing adventure. As fate would have it, she found herself seated next to a kind-hearted retired teacher named Mrs. Evans. A chance encounter that would prove to be a pivotal moment in Alex's journey.

Mrs. Evans, with her warm smile and gentle demeanor, immediately struck up a conversation with Alex. They talked about their respective reasons for traveling to New Orleans, and Mrs. Evans shared stories of her own past adventures. Sensing Alex's restlessness, Mrs. Evans reached into her bag and pulled out a beautifully bound journal.

"I think this might be of great use to you, dear," Mrs. Evans said, her eyes twinkling with wisdom. "Documenting your journey can be cathartic and enlightening. It allows you to reflect on the lessons learned and the growth experienced along the way."

Grateful for the unexpected gift, Alex accepted the journal with a sense of reverence. She vowed to take Mrs. Evans' advice to heart and diligently record her thoughts, emotions, and the events that would unfold during her journey.

As the train continued its rhythmic chugging, Alex noticed two other passengers in the adjacent seats. Maria, a resilient single mother, and Leo, a talented musician, were engaged in an animated conversation. Their stories of struggle, resilience, and hope resonated deeply with Alex.

Maria, with her unwavering determination and unwavering love for her child, shared her own journey of overcoming adversity as a single parent. Her muted strength, laced in her words, inspired Alex to face her own challenges head-on.

Leo shared his passion for music and how it became his beacon of hope during the darkest times of his life. Through his melodies, he found solace, joy, and the ability to connect with others on a profound level. His story reminded Alex of the transformative power of art and how it could heal even the most broken souls.

As the train sped towards its destination, Alex felt a newfound sense of purpose and determination. The encounters with Mrs. Evans, Maria, and Leo had bolstered her resolve to embark on this journey with an open heart and a willingness to embrace the unknown.

Alex held Mrs. Evans' journal. The stories of Maria and Leo resonated deeply. She knew this trip to New Orleans would be more than physical; it would be a journey of self-discovery.

Chapter 3: New Beginnings

Arriving in New Orleans, Alex felt both exhilarated and overwhelmed. She found temporary shelter at a hostel and relentlessly searched for a job. Eventually, she discovered an old bookstore, "Whispering Pages," and convinced the owner, Mr. Thompson, to let her work for lodging.

Chapter 4: Rediscovery

As Alex settled into her new role, she rekindled her passion for writing. She started a blog, "Life in a Suitcase," chronicling her experiences. Her heartfelt posts resonated with readers, slowly building a loyal following.

She found joy in minor victories, like making friends with locals and mastering the art of navigating the bustling city.

Chapter 5: Community and Connection

The bookstore became a sanctuary for Alex, a place where she could escape the chaos of everyday life. With its cozy atmosphere and shelves filled with books of all genres, it provided a haven for her to retreat to whenever she needed solace.

It wasn't long before Alex's passion for literature and community led her to transform the bookstore into more than just a place to buy books. She started organizing events, ranging from book signings to literary discussions, which brought together people from all social classes. These events not only highlighted the diverse interests and talents of the community but also created a space for meaningful connections to be forged.

One of these connections was with Sophie, a quirky artist who stumbled upon the bookstore one rainy afternoon. Sophie's vibrant personality and unique outlook energized the bookstore. She became a fixture, hosting art workshops and displaying her art.

Another meaningful connection was with Marcus, a kind-hearted chef who owned a nearby restaurant. Their paths crossed during a food and literature event that Alex organized, and they quickly discovered a shared love for storytelling through both words and flavors. Marcus began hosting cooking demonstrations at the bookstore, displaying his culinary skills and sharing his recipes with the eager attendees.

As these connections grew deeper, the sense of belonging that Alex felt within the bookstore expanded beyond its physical walls. It became a tight-knit community, where people supported and uplifted each other. A renewed sense of purpose and belonging revitalized Alex. This reminded her of the power of human connection and the value of creating a welcoming environment for all.

Chapter 6: The Setback

Just as stability seemed within reach, Mr. Thompson received news that the bookstore was facing closure. Desperate to save her sanctuary, Alex rallied the community, organizing a benefit concert and a fundraising campaign. With the support of her friends and readers, they raised enough funds to save the bookstore.

Chapter 7: Triumph and Transformation

The success of the fundraiser, organized by Alex, brought her blog to the attention of a prominent publisher in the industry. Recognizing the potential in Alex's captivating storytelling and inspiring journey, the publisher approached her with an enticing book deal. Filled with a mix of excitement and gratitude, Alex couldn't help but reflect on the incredible progress she had made in her life.

From facing immense hardships and starting with nothing but a single suitcase, she had now become a symbol of resilience and reinvention. Her story had the power to touch the hearts and minds of people from all levels of society, becoming a shining beacon of hope for those seeking inspiration.

Alex's experiences revealed that true wealth lies not in material possessions, but in rich experiences, meaningful connections, and cherished memories.

Epilogue: A New Chapter

Years later, Alex, a once struggling writer, stood before a packed auditorium filled with eager listeners. Confidently, she shared an excerpt from her bestselling memoir. It detailed her journey from despair to triumph, a journey she viewed with accomplishment and gratitude. The audience hung on her every word, captivated by her raw honesty and vulnerability.

As she closed the book, a wave of emotions washed over her, and she couldn't help but feel a profound sense of fulfillment. Looking out at the diverse sea of faces, she realized her story had resonated with countless others who had faced their own trials and tribulations. It was a moment of realization for Alex, as she came to understand that her words had the power to inspire, heal, and uplift.

Her life, which had once seemed confined and limited, had now expanded beyond her wildest dreams. The applause that erupted from the audience was not just a recognition of her literary achievement, but a heartfelt tribute to the transformative power of the human spirit. As Alex took a deep breath and soaked in the room's energy, she knew she had fulfilled her life's purpose.

There, behind the wooden podium, illuminated by the soft glow of the overhead lights, was her only suitcase, a worn and weathered traveler's companion. Its sturdy exterior bore the marks of countless journeys, each scratch and scuff telling a story of adventure and discovery.

The suitcase, faithfully by her side throughout her academic pursuits, now carried within its depths a treasure trove of knowledge and inspiration. Nestled among the neatly folded clothes and toiletries were her meticulously handwritten notes, carefully crafted over countless late nights and early mornings.

These notes, a testament to her dedication and thirst for knowledge, were a lifeline to her success. Alongside the notes, several well-worn books found their place within the suitcase's confines. Each book, dog-eared and annotated, represented a cherished resource and a constant source of intellectual stimulation.

These beloved companions had accompanied her through the labyrinth of academia, providing guidance and enlightenment along the way. As she stood before the podium, her only suitcase served as a tangible reminder of the countless hours of hard work and determination that had brought her to this moment. It was a symbol of her unwavering commitment to her studies and her unyielding pursuit of excellence.

16

Living Sermons

A warm and comforting glow filled the small country church, created by the morning sun filtering through the stained-glass windows. The congregation stood there eagerly, their faces a mix of anticipation and reverence, coming to be inspired by the weekly sermon's uplifting message.

Among them was Harry, a man in his late thirties with a heavy burden on his weary shoulders. It had been just a few months since he lost his job abruptly, and it had sent shockwaves through his already fragile sense of stability.

Now, as he sits amongst his fellow worshippers, he grapples with the overwhelming uncertainty of his future. The familiar hymns and the comfortable atmosphere of the church provide him solace and a temporary respite from the constant anxieties that plague his mind. As the minister stepped up to the pulpit, Harry's attention shifted, hopeful that today's sermon would offer him the guidance and reassurance he so desperately sought.

As the service began, Pastor Cindy stood at the pulpit, a serene smile on her face. People knew her for her eloquent sermons, which always left the congregation feeling inspired and uplifted. Today, however, was different. There was a sense of anticipation in the air as the members of the church settled into their seats, eager to see what Pastor Cindy had in store for them. Her reputation as a talented speaker attracted a large crowd, filling the pews with people from all levels of society.

As the room grew muted, Pastor Cindy took a moment to survey the faces before her. The collective curiosity and intrigue emanating from the congregation was something she could feel. It was as if they were all hanging on her every word, ready to embark on a new spiritual journey.

With a gentle clearing of her throat, Pastor Cindy addressed the congregation. Her voice was calm and steady, filled with quiet confidence that commanded attention. "Today, I won't be delivering a traditional sermon," she declared, her eyes scanning the room. The congregation shifted in their seats; their curiosity piqued. They had come expecting a typical Sunday service, but Pastor Cindy had something entirely different in mind.

Instead of launching into a sermon, Pastor Cindy revealed her intention to share a story. It was a story that would transcend the boundaries of mere words, a narrative that would awaken the senses and touch the hearts of those who listened. She wanted to show the congregation how to truly see, not just hear, the messages conveyed through sermons.

The gentle rustling of the trees outside was the only sound heard as the church fell silent. Anticipation filled the atmosphere, as if the air itself promised something extraordinary.

Pastor Cindy, a woman with decades of experience in guiding her congregation, stood at the pulpit with a serene smile. Her eyes sparkled with wisdom and compassion; her voice soothed the hearts of those listening with a soothing tone that captivated them.

The congregation, a diverse group of individuals seeking spiritual nourishment, leaned forward in their pews, their eyes fixed on her with unwavering attention. Each member carried his or her own hopes and desires, ready to embark on this new and unique spiritual experience that Pastor Cindy had promised.

The stained-glass windows bathed the room in a kaleidoscope of colors, casting a warm and ethereal glow upon the faces of the faithful. The air was thick with anticipation, a palpable energy that seemed to vibrate within the walls of the church. They knew that within these sacred walls, something transformative was about to unfold. Anxiously, they awaited the words that would touch their souls and ignite a renewed sense of purpose within them.

The soft rustling of leaves outside punctuated the stillness of the moment, as if nature itself were holding its breath in reverence. In this sacred space, Pastor Cindy's serene smile remained in place, radiating a sense of peace and assurance that calmed the restless hearts of her congregation. The stage was ready, and the congregation waited to receive the spiritual nourishment they sought. Pastor Cindy then, smiling, reminisced.

Years ago, after seminary, I served in a small Midwestern town. It was there, amidst the simplicity and tight-knit community, that I had the privilege of meeting a remarkable woman named Mary. Although she wasn't particularly religious in the conventional sense, Mary embodied the very essence of what it means to live out one's faith in the world.

Mary, a kind-hearted widow in her late fifties, lived in a cozy cottage on the outskirts of town. Her life was humble and unassuming, devoid of any ostentatious displays of wealth or material possessions. She didn't feel the need to attend church services religiously or proselytize her beliefs to others. Instead, Mary's faith manifested itself through her selfless actions and unwavering compassion for her fellow human beings.

Every single day, without fail, Mary would make her way to the local nursing home, armed with homemade meals and a heart full of love. She would spend hours sitting with the elderly residents, listening to their stories, and offering them comfort in their twilight years. Her presence brought warmth and joy to their lives, and many would eagerly expect her daily visits, knowing that Mary's kindness would brighten their day.

But Mary's benevolence didn't stop there. She selflessly dedicated her time and energy to volunteer at the local food bank, tirelessly sorting and distributing food to those in need. With a warm smile and a gentle touch, she would provide not just nourishment but also a sense of dignity and hope to those who found themselves in desperate circumstances. Mary's unwavering commitment to serving others was truly an inspiration to all who knew her.

Though her faith may have been quiet and unassuming, Mary's actions spoke volumes. She embodied the very essence of compassion, love, and selflessness that lies at the core of any sincere religious belief.

Pastor Cindy and the entire community learned from her example that living one's faith means more than attending church or saying prayers; it's about making a tangible difference in others' lives. Mary's legacy continues to resonate in the hearts of all who were fortunate enough to witness her unwavering devotion to the well-being of her fellow human beings.

Harry listened intently, feeling a deep sense of connection to Mary's story. As Pastor Cindy spoke about Mary's journey of faith and the impact it had on her life, Harry couldn't help but recall his own beloved grandmother. She had lived a life of remarkable grace and humility, always putting others before herself. Despite never actively preaching, her actions spoke volumes about her unwavering faith and love for humanity.

One of the most vivid memories Harry had of his grandmother was her dedication to helping those in need. She would spend countless hours stitching together beautiful quilts, pouring her heart and soul into every stitch. She did not make these quilts for her own comfort or enjoyment; they were made for nursing home residents. Harry admired how his grandmother never sought recognition or praise for her selfless acts. She simply believed in the power of small acts of kindness and the impact they could have on someone's life.

One phrase that always resonated with Harry was his grandmother's favorite saying: "Let your light shine before others." This quote, derived from Matthew 5:16 in the Bible, encapsulated the essence of his grandmother's approach to life. She believed that by living a life of genuine kindness and love, one could inspire and uplift others. Her light gleamed through her actions, touching the lives of many in her community.

As Mary's story unfolded, Harry couldn't help but feel a renewed sense of gratitude for his grandmother's influence in his life. Her quiet generosity and unwavering faith had left an indelible mark on his heart. Inspired by both Mary's journey and his grandmother's legacy, Harry felt compelled to embrace his own faith more fully and seek opportunities to let his light shine before others.

Pastor Cindy continued her discourse by telling the congregation about a harsh winter, a relentless snowstorm abruptly overtaking the small town. Roads became impassable, isolating the residents within their homes. However, amidst this chaos, a remarkable individual named Mary emerged as a beacon of hope. Her unwavering determination and selflessness during this crisis not only provided immediate relief to those in need but also ignited a spirit of unity and compassion within the entire community.

As the snowstorm blanketed the town, its inhabitants found themselves trapped within the confines of their homes. The severity of the storm led to a shortage of supplies, leaving many vulnerable and anxious about their well-being. However, Mary, a resident known for her kindness and community spirit, sprang into action without hesitation.

Undeterred by the treacherous conditions, Mary embarked on a courageous journey through the snow-covered streets. Equipped with a backpack filled with essential supplies, she made it her mission to reach out to those who could not buy the provisions for themselves. Mary's unwavering determination and selflessness became a ray of hope in the otherwise gloomy landscape.

Word of Mary's efforts quickly spread throughout the community, inspiring others to join her noble cause. Soon, a network of volunteers emerged, driven by a shared desire to help those most affected by the snowstorm. Together, they formed a makeshift relief team, diligently working to deliver much-needed food, medicine, and warmth to their neighbors in need.

The sight of Mary and her team braving the elements to help others stirred a sense of unity and solidarity among the townspeople. People who had never interacted before worked side by side, bound by a common purpose. The community became a tight-knit support system, with individuals offering their time, resources, and expertise to assist their fellow residents.

Through the tireless efforts of Mary and the collective response of the community, the impact of the snowstorm was mitigated. A compassionate society embraced the isolated and vulnerable, refusing to let them suffer alone. The actions of one person had transformed a crisis into an opportunity for the community to rally together, reminding everyone of the strength and resilience that lies within them.

The severe snowstorm that had initially threatened to divide the town became the catalyst for unity and compassion, thanks to the selflessness and determination of Mary. Her willingness to brave the elements and assist those in need inspired an entire community to come together and support one another. This remarkable show of solidarity proves the power of kindness. Even during hardship, unity brings strength and hope.

Pastor Cindy's words visibly moved the congregation. Her words painted a vivid picture of Mary's life, illustrating the profound impact of living one's faith. Pastor Cindy, softening her voice, continued her sermon.

But Mary's story doesn't end there. She faced her own share of hardships. Despite battling a chronic illness that often left her weak and in pain, Mary never allowed her own suffering to overshadow her dedication to helping others. She experienced financial struggles, often living on a tight budget, but she never hesitated to give whatever she could to those in need. Mary's life was a living sermon, a testament to the power of kindness and compassion. She showed us that true strength lies not in the absence of difficulties, but in how we respond to them with love and selflessness.

Harry felt a lump in his throat as he reflected on his own struggles. Mary's story resonated with him deeply, reminding him of the strength and resilience that comes from helping others.

Pastor Cindy then concluded her sermon.

Mary taught me that sermons aren't just words spoken from a pulpit. They are the actions we take every day, how we treat others, and the love we share. Her life was a beacon of light, guiding others through their darkest moments.

Mary, a devoted member of our congregation for over 30 years, embodied the true essence of faith and compassion. Despite facing numerous personal struggles, she consistently showed unwavering kindness, generosity, and a genuine concern for the well-being of those around her. Whether it was offering a listening ear to someone in need or organizing community outreach programs, Mary's commitment to making a positive difference was unparalleled.

She inspired and encouraged her church family. Her example teaches us that sermons are about more than words; they're about impacting lives. We will forever cherish Mary's legacy as we strive to emulate her selflessness and be a guiding light for those in need. Her memory will endure, inspiring us to live with love and compassion.

As the service ended, Harry felt a renewed sense of purpose. Inspired by Mary's example, he resolved to live his life as a living sermon, embracing kindness and compassion in everything he did. This decision led Harry on a transformative journey that brought fulfillment, meaning, and a deeper understanding of faith.

Harry began volunteering at the local shelter, recognizing the urgent need for support in his community. He dedicated his time and skills to help those in need, offering a helping hand and a listening ear. Whether it was serving meals, organizing donations, or providing emotional support, Harry made it his mission to make a positive impact on the lives of others.

Realizing the importance of building strong relationships, Harry reached out to his friends and family, offering support and encouragement. He understood that sometimes a simple act of kindness or a heartfelt conversation could make a world of difference. Harry became a pillar of strength for those around him, offering unwavering support during their times of struggle and celebrating their successes.

Through his selfless actions, Harry experienced a profound transformation in his own life. He found a new job that aligned with his values and allowed him to make a difference in the lives of others. However, the true reward came from the inner fulfillment and meaning he discovered. Harry realized that by embodying his life as a living sermon, he could tap into a sense of purpose and joy that transcended material achievements.

Harry's dedication and selflessness did not go unnoticed. As he continued to lead a life of kindness and compassion, he became an inspiration to those around him. His actions spoke louder than words, showing others the true essence of faith. By embodying the values he held dear, Harry encouraged others to examine their own lives and consider the impact they could have on their communities.

Harry's decision to embody the essence of a living sermon transformed his life in ways he never imagined. Through volunteering at the local shelter, supporting friends and family, and finding personal fulfillment, he discovered the true essence of faith. Harry's journey serves as a reminder that the power of kindness and compassion lies not in the words we speak, but in the lives we lead. His story continues to inspire others to embrace these values and make a positive difference in the world around them.

Harry's story reminded him of the parable of the Good Samaritan (Luke 10:25-37). He recalled how the Samaritan helped a stranger in need, despite their differences. It was a powerful example of living out one's faith through actions, not just words.

17

Finding Peace in Turbulent Times

I tell a story of a young mother who experienced the difficulties of looking after her children alone after the death of her husband. She was depressed and overwhelmed with the responsibilities of taking care of her children and turned to a community group that met at a church for help. The links she formed, and the similar experiences within the group, gave her a sense of belonging and encouragement. By depending on other people and helping them in return, she could find peace and strengthen her character.

Several years ago, I knew a man who was an artist who lost his job because of an economic crisis. His depression and hopelessness about the future led him to rekindle his love for painting. He could express his fears, hopes and dreams through his art. The act of creating became for him a way to express his feelings. His emotions found a release in the brush strokes that he made. It was a process of healing and discovery for him. His journey inspired people in his community to resort to their creativity to solve the problem of finding peace during the time of crisis.

I recall counseling with a man who, after a painful breakup, discovered the healing power of nature. He went for a walk in the nearby forests and parks as much as he could, and he found comfort in the natural environment. Nature offered him solace. A walk in the woods, listening to birdsong, and feeling the earth—these simple things brought him refuge. Eventually, these walks served a dual purpose: they enabled him to process the grief of losing his love and they also cultivated within him a deeper awareness of himself and his surroundings.

People today are looking for peace in a world where things are very unstable. The constant barrage of negative news, coupled with the ongoing pandemic and numerous other social and political issues, has understandably led to widespread stress and anxiety among many individuals. Many individuals are actively seeking methods and practices to cultivate inner peace and tranquility, striving for a sense of calm and serenity within their own minds and spirits. To cope with stress and enhance their mental clarity, they are exploring and incorporating meditation, mindfulness, and yoga into their lives.

People are now returning to nature and outdoor activities to find peace and to be alone and reflect on themselves. Some are now into gardening or hiking while others are spending more time in the natural environment to find peace. People are also in search of peace through interaction and relationships. Besides their physical health, they prioritize their mental and emotional well-being, actively cultivating supportive relationships with positive individuals who provide encouragement and assistance during challenging periods. The search for peace has become one of the most important concerns of people in the contemporary world and everyone is looking for diverse ways to achieve it.

Philippians 4:6-7: "Be careful for nothing; but in every thing by prayer and supplication with thanksgiving let your requests be made known unto God. And the peace of God, which passeth all understanding, shall keep your hearts and minds through Christ Jesus."

This passage instructs us to cease fretting, instead focusing our anxieties through prayer and supplication, entrusting our worries to God's care and seeking divine guidance through petition. It is important to come to God with a heart full of thanks, with gratefulness for all His blessings. Thus, we open the door for the peace of God to come into our lives, a peace that is beyond our comprehension. This divine peace protects our hearts and minds in Christ Jesus and does so even in the face of uncertainty and difficulty. This verse tells us how we can relieve our anxiety and worry if we decide to offer them to God and believe that He is in control. God's presence offers comfort during life's changes and uncertainties. We don't have to face them alone.

Isaiah 26:3-4: "Thou wilt keep him in perfect peace, whose mind is stayed on thee: because he trusteth in thee. Trust ye in the Lord for ever: for in the Lord JEHOVAH is everlasting strength."

Isaiah 26:3-4 reveals to us the peace that we can find in God. These verses highlight the importance of having a powerful spirit, a spirit of faith and trust in God. The reason for this action is that it allows us to experience the impenetrable peace of God, a truly protective and unbreakable shield against life's troubles. This passage provides solace and comfort, especially to individuals who desire to rely on God's unwavering presence and place their trust in Him within the complexities of this world.

John 14:27: "Peace I leave with you, my peace I give unto you: not as the world giveth, give I unto you. Let not your heart be troubled, neither let it be afraid."

In the comforting and beautiful passage of John 14:27, Jesus speaks words of comfort to his disciples, addressing their confusion and fear. Jesus, in promising his followers peace that surpasses all worldly under-standing, assures them that even though he will soon depart, this peace will remain with them. Amid turmoil and suffering, it is a peace that is unique and only God can provide. Addressing their concerns, he declared that worry and fear were unnecessary; his victory over the world enabled him to offer them his hard-earned peace.

The enduring comfort and meaning found in the words of Jesus remain powerfully relevant for believers facing the present crises. Amidst the societal decay surrounding us, these individuals crucially remind us of the peace and comfort found through faith in Jesus, offering sanctuary from the ever-increasing turmoil. This message encourages us to hold fast to his promises, to take our anxieties to him, and to seek refuge in the embrace of his love.

Psalm 46:1-2: "God is our refuge and strength, a very present help in trouble. Therefore will not we fear, though the earth be remove, and though the mountains be carried into the midst of the sea."

Among the many encouraging passages found within the Book of Psalms in the Bible, Psalm 46:1-2 is notably prominent for its message of comfort and strength. Providing encouragement, a sense of God's presence and protection, and comfort to those facing hardship, it serves as a valuable resource.

Verse 1: "God is our refuge and strength, an ever-present help in trouble."

The psalm's opening verse highlights God's unchanging nature. He is a constant protector and source of strength for those who seek Him. The word 'refuge' means safety and protection, while the word 'strength' means power and help. This verse potently reminds us that amidst life's trials and tribulations, we can discover solace and peace through faith and a steadfast connection with God's unwavering presence. This verse portrays God as always there to help. The phrase "ever-present help in time of trouble" emphasizes His constant support during hardship.

Verse 2: "Therefore we will not fear, though the earth give way and the mountains fall into the heart of the sea."

Based on the premise of the firm support of God, the psalmist calls on people to have faith and to believe. Though the psalmist's metaphors of a collapsing earth and sinking mountains suggest chaos, those who trust in God have nothing to fear. This serves as a powerful example, demonstrating the ability to maintain strength and confidence by relying on, and trusting in, the power and protection that God provides. Despite the darkness, the message conveys hope. Trust in God's authority provides comfort, no matter the circumstances.

Psalm 46:1-2 provides a magnificent and reassuring message about God's steadfast presence and sheltering protection during times of trouble, offering believers a source of comfort and strength. The message is clear: there is no need for fear because God's presence offers our spirits a refuge and assures us of His unwavering support. This passage has been a source of comfort and encouragement to countless people who have used these words throughout the years. It is therefore possible to rely on God's strength and seek His shelter and stay strong.

I am inspired by the story of my friend, Sarah, who found solace and peace during a difficult phase of her life. Sarah's story began when she felt her job was overwhelming and that her personal issues were adding to the pressure. She was depressed and burned out and she turned to mindfulness and meditation in order to regain her balance and find her center.

With no knowledge of meditation techniques, Sarah started on her new journey with an empty mind ready to learn. She started by taking a few minutes each day to practice some breathing exercises and guided meditation. At first it was strange and foreign, but she persisted, knowing that change was not instantaneous and that it takes arduous work.

As the weeks progressed, Sarah noticed some changes in her attitude and overall health. The place of stillness and introspection that she had created for herself was a sanctuary amid the storm that was her daily life. Through each breath and each meditation session, she became increasingly conscious of her own internal landscape of thoughts and emotions, fostering a deeper self-awareness.

Through the practices of mindfulness and meditation, Sarah discovered effective coping mechanisms that enabled her to navigate the increasingly hard challenges she faced in both her professional and personal life. The pressures that had at one time seemed overwhelming were now not as overwhelming since she could manage them with a calm and composed mind. Peace and acceptance gradually replaced the negative feelings and the stress that used to control. With the help of the verses in Philippians 4:6, she could change her outlook on life, and it changed her in a way that was very noticeable.

This narrative recounts the life-changing journey of my friend Sarah. The practices of mindfulness and meditation catalyzed her transformation, offering a valuable and universally applicable lesson. Though the world is turbulent, inner peace and biblical wisdom can offer solace and perspective during life's challenges. Achieving calmness and recognizing one's inner strength and courage is possible, which will then allow one to approach life's challenges with both courage and clarity of thought.

If you are experiencing turbulent times, then seek the strong rock that is Jesus Christ. In the world of uncertainty and chaos, Jesus brings comfort and support. Whatever the issues that you may have, he will listen to your cry and concerns. He is full of love and compassion, which brings comfort and direction during the time of trouble. He is infinite in wisdom and can give wisdom and direction in the storm's light. In these uncertain times, faith in Jesus offers comfort, peace, and hope. It provides a solid foundation for life. Place your trust and reliance on Him and allow Him to guide and create a path for you, leading you towards your future.

18

The Honeymoon Period

<figure>divider ornament</figure>

Pastor Mark, a charismatic and insightful speaker, delivered an engaging sermon today on Luke 4 at First United Methodist. The congregation eagerly gathered to listen to his words of wisdom and spiritual guidance.

With a warm smile and a contagious enthusiasm, Pastor Mark captivated the audience from the moment he stepped into the pulpit. His sermon focused on the profound teachings found in the fourth chapter of the Gospel of Luke. He skillfully unpacked the passage, exploring its historical context and highlighting its relevance to the lives of the listeners. Drawing from his extensive knowledge of biblical scholarship, Pastor Mark offered profound insights and practical applications for the modern-day Christian. His eloquent delivery and passion for the Scriptures made the sermon not only informative but also deeply inspiring.

Throughout his message, Pastor Mark emphasized the importance of faith, perseverance, and the life-changing power of God's Word. He encouraged the congregation to reflect on their own lives and to seek a deeper understanding of their faith through personal study and prayer.

His message was about the honeymoon period in Luke 4. In his sermon, Pastor Mark explored the concept of the honeymoon period as it relates to the events described in Luke 4 of the Bible. Jesus reads the scrolls and then sits to deliver the message (as was the custom). Jesus's message was very brief and emphasizes that He is the message for the day.

The passage in Luke 4 recounts the beginning of Jesus' public ministry after being baptized and tempted in the wilderness. Pastor Mark explained the importance of this moment, showing how the people reacted to Jesus with excitement, curiosity, and admiration. This period of enthusiastic support and adoration, often referred to as the honeymoon period, is a common experience in various aspects of life, including relationships, careers, and even spirituality.

Pastor Mark drew parallels between the honeymoon period in Luke 4 and the subsequent challenges and rejection Jesus faced throughout His ministry. Through this exploration, he encouraged the congregation to reflect on their own spiritual journeys and consider how they respond when the initial excitement fades and difficulties arise. The sermon aimed to inspire a deeper understanding of the commitment and perseverance required to follow Jesus beyond the honeymoon period and into a lifelong relationship with Him.

Renee and I had a wedding I vividly remember. I can still picture the quaint little 1972 VW Beetle parked just outside the charming white wood-framed church where we exchanged our vows. The sun was gleaming, casting a warm glow on the vibrant flowers adorning the entrance.

It was a perfect day for a wedding, and I couldn't contain my excitement, knowing that our honeymoon in Chattanooga, Tennessee, awaited us. However, as we were preparing to leave, panic suddenly gripped me - the car keys were nowhere to be found. It didn't take long for me to realize my absent-mindedness - I had left them in the car! Despite this slight hiccup, both of us were brimming with joy and anticipation for the journey ahead.

Now, as I reflect on that memorable day, I can hardly believe that 52 years have passed since. We experienced countless milestones and adventures during that time. Two beautiful children blessed our lives, and we've joyfully watched them grow into remarkable adults.

Along the way, our family has expanded further with the addition of two precious grandchildren, who bring endless delight to our lives.

Professionally, we have dedicated ourselves to serving the community, having had the privilege of ministering to over twenty different churches throughout the years. Our journey has also led us to share our musical talents at numerous weddings and funerals, providing solace and joy during both joyous and sorrowful moments.

Looking back, it's astounding to consider the myriad experiences and memories that have shaped our lives over the past five decades. Time has brought challenges, but Renee and I remain steadfast in our love and bond, a constant source of strength and comfort. As we celebrate this momentous anniversary, we can't help but feel immense gratitude for the life we have built together and the countless blessings we have received. Here's to the next chapter of our journey, filled with even more love, laughter, and cherished moments.

Despite that, our marriage hasn't been without its difficulties. I don't really believe that any marriage is perfect. Couples disagree on various issues, such as finances, parenting styles, and even household chores. Inevitably, during these disagreements, couples may say hurtful things to each other in the heat of the moment. This can lead to resentment and strained communication.

Both partners may occasionally exhibit behaviors such as pouting or withdrawing when they don't get their way, which can further strain the relationship. Over time, couples can become indifferent towards each other's needs and desires, leading to a lack of emotional connection and intimacy. It's natural for marriages to face challenges. Active conflict resolution, improved communication, and nurturing the emotional bond are essential for a fulfilling relationship.

The honeymoon period Jesus experienced on the occasion in Luke 4 refers to the early stage of his ministry, immediately after his baptism and temptation in the wilderness. In this chapter of the Bible, Jesus returns to his hometown of Nazareth and goes to the synagogue on the Sabbath day. The synagogue leader gave him the opportunity to read from the scroll of the prophet Isaiah and deliver a sermon. His wise, authoritative speech and teaching amazed and impressed the people in the synagogue. They speak well of him and marvel at his ability to perform miracles.

It is a period of excitement and adoration for Jesus, as the people see him as a powerful and wise figure who brings hope and redemption. However, this honeymoon period is short-lived, as Jesus soon faces opposition and rejection from some of the same people who initially praised him. This episode in Luke 4 sets the stage for the challenges and conflicts Jesus will encounter throughout his ministry.

How eagerly we follow a leader until they demand that we "feed" his sheep! This statement shows that people willingly and enthusiastically follow a leader until that leader makes them responsible for others. Initially, a leader's charisma, vision, and guidance motivate followers, who eagerly embrace their ideas and directives.

However, when the leader expects their followers to serve and support the needs of others, it can become a challenging task. The demand to "feed" the leader's sheep implies the obligation to provide nourishment, guidance, and support to those under their care. This demand often requires sacrifice, dedication, and a deep sense of responsibility. Here, the followers test their genuine commitment and character as they decide whether to meet the leader's expectations and care for others. The willingness to serve and support others is a defining characteristic of effective leaders and followers alike.

The first four years of our marriage were fantastic! We had built a firm foundation of love and shared experiences. We enjoyed exploring novel places together, trying new activities, and simply spending quality time with each other. Our bond seemed unbreakable, and we couldn't imagine life getting any better. And then Angie came along and took up most of our attention. Her birth gave us additional responsibilities and duties we had never had before.

Suddenly, our focus shifted from just the two of us to the needs and well-being of our precious baby girl. We were on a learning curve, navigating the uncharted waters of parenthood, and it often felt like the curve was winning. Sleepless nights, endless diaper changes, and the constant juggling act of balancing work and family life became our new reality.

But amidst the chaos, there were moments of pure joy and overwhelming love that made it all worthwhile. We marveled at Angie's first smile, her tiny fingers gripping ours, and her infectious laughter that could brighten even the darkest days.

We tested our relationship but learned to lean on each other for support and to share the joys and challenges of raising a child together. Despite the inevitable trials, we were determined to make our marriage thrive in this new chapter of our lives. We embraced the changes and welcomed the opportunity to grow as individuals and as a couple. Our love for each other only deepened as we witnessed the incredible transformation of our family. The first four years were only the beginning. We've been on a beautiful journey of love, laughter, and building a fulfilling life for our child. And four years later Jonathan came along.

A honeymoon never has to end. In fact, we should have a honeymoon each year that we are married. It makes our lives more exciting and reminds us of that very first honeymoon.

Jesus's followers were eager at first, and the honeymoon was on. His teachings, miracles, and the promise of eternal life captivated them. Jesus's followers experienced excitement and wonder in the early days as they witnessed His power and authority. However, challenges soon tested their commitment to Him. Jesus challenged each of them to go into the world and make disciples, spreading His message of love and redemption.

This task was not an easy one. It required sacrifice, selflessness, and a willingness to serve others. The disciples were called to offer themselves as living sacrifices, putting the needs of others before their own. They were to be a light in a mysterious world, showing compassion and kindness to those who were hurting and in need.

This labor-intensive discipleship could sometimes bring even the most enthusiastic follower down. The demands were high, and the road was not always easy. But a true disciple, one who had truly grasped the depth of Jesus's love and the significance of His mission, would follow Him to the end. They understood following Jesus was not about personal gain or comfort. It was about surrendering their lives to Him and walking in His footsteps, no matter the cost.

As Pastor Mark concluded his sermon, there was a tangible sense of spiritual upliftment in the sanctuary. The congregation left with renewed hope and a strengthened commitment to live out their faith in their daily lives. Pastor Mark's sermon, based on Luke 4, powerfully reminded listeners of the Bible's enduring wisdom. The impact was profound.

19

"What Ifs" and Regrets

Should have, could have, and would have been are expressions used in discussing missed opportunities or regrets. These expressions highlight alternative courses of action one could have pursued. 'Should have' means that something was the right or expected thing to do, but it was not done. 'Could have' shows available possibilities or choices that remained unchosen or unpursued. "Would have," a counterfactual, describes an event that didn't happen, with the author imagining a different result based on hypothetical actions. These expressions are used to express a feeling of regret, to own up to a mistake, or to concede that one has missed a chance. One can use them anywhere, including interpersonal relationships, careers, or even history.

In the late 1960s, one of my closest friends found himself at a crossroads in his life. He was a music enthusiast and had spent several years developing his guitar skills to an elevated level. It was during this time that destiny had brought to him a wonderful chance—a chance to join a band that was going on an exciting tour in the United States. But life had just taken a new turn for him; he had just gotten married to his love and had started a job, a dream job that was going to provide him financial security and happiness. Recognizing the temptation that the band presented to my friend, he turned down the band's kind offer to stay committed to his new life. He wouldn't have known this decision was pivotal to his whole musical life.

Several years later, my friend stood by his baby's crib, listening to the radio as the air filled with the sound of the new wave of rock and roll. Listening to the radio, he heard the very band he'd rejected achieve nationwide and international fame.

At that moment, he told me that, while the feelings that were stirring in his heart were not negative, he could not help but feel a certain amount of regret for what might have been. Although he could not help but feel a tinge of regret for the missed opportunity, he also felt content and happy with the decision he had made. Life had brought him a few choices, and he had chosen the right one—one that would lead him to happiness and satisfaction in life. He continues to play his guitar and works on improving his craft, but his band days are through. He plays the music of the sixties for his wife and two children.

Oh, the "what ifs!" I wish I could have attended college and learned what I wanted to. What if I had done everything I wanted to do in life? Life is full of ifs and buts. What if we had made different decisions? What if we had taken a different path? It is possible to get stuck in your head thinking about these things and feeling like you don't know which way to turn.

However, staring at what ifs can also limit us from living in the present and looking ahead. It makes sense to reflect on past choices and find middle ground between them and what lies ahead. That is why it is possible to gain experience, make the right decisions, and live a purposeful life.

This is how we are. We often reflect on alternative realities. Considering the various consequences is instinctive for humans.

Looking back at the decisions we have made in the past allows us to gain knowledge and make better decisions in the future.

Sometimes, imagining different outcomes can help us feel like we have some control over what's happened in the past.

What-ifs and feelings of loss or futility characterize regret. Some regrets are:

Educational Choices: "I regret not completing my university education."

Missed Opportunities: "I regret not using my spare time better when I had the chance."

Relationship Decisions: "I regret not spending more time with my loved ones." Although feeling sorry for what-ifs and regrets is a part of human nature, it is necessary to not let these thoughts control one's mind. Instead, we can use these thoughts as valuable tools for reflection, learning, and personal growth. We do, therefore, get to be shaped by our experiences, but they should not define us. The actions we take in the present moment really determine the course of our lives and the direction we will take in the future.

Here are a few things that we can do to improve our lives in this respect:

1. Embrace Reflection:

To harness the power of reflection, it is important to embrace the process rather than avoid it. When we allow our minds to wander to the what-ifs and regrets, we are offering ourselves a way to self-discovery and understanding. This introspection assists us in understanding the decisions we have made, the reasons that shape our decisions, and the actions we perform. It is an art that can help one grow and develop as a person.

2. Learn from Our Mistakes:

Folly or missed opportunities usually cause regrets. Rather than reverting to the regrets, it is possible to choose to consider them as learning experiences. This way, we can determine the cause of the failure and learn the lessons that lead to our regrets. This new understanding enables us to make better decisions and do things that may not lead us to making the same mistakes again.

3. Shape a Positive Mindset:

When thinking about the events that have taken place, it is crucial to have a positive mindset. Rather than focusing on the negative, it is possible to switch the attention to the positive outcomes or the personal development. It is also possible to change our perception and use our time to develop a more positive outlook on life.

4. Acting in the Present:

Reflection is a remarkably effective tool; however, it is actions that are taken in the present that are most significant in shaping one's life. With the knowledge gained from reflection, we can make deliberate choices aligning with our values and goals. Every action we take has the capability of affecting our lives and the lives of those around us.

In his quest for spiritual excellence, the apostle Paul reveals his dedication in his letter to the Philippians. In Philippians 3:13-14 Paul admits he has not yet attained the spiritual maturity that he longs for, but he declares he has not lost his passion to progress, looking ahead, forgetting what lies behind him, and pressing towards the goal that is before him. We can usefully apply this passage to challenge believers to look forward and keep striving on their journey of faith.

Here Paul announces his current situation and thus does not consider himself to have taken hold of the spiritual growth for which he yearns. This admission of imperfection is a testament to Paul's humility; he realizes that there is always room for growth and improvement in one's relationship with God.

The apostle then continues to the next point, which is to put away the past. By "forgetting what is behind," Paul emphasizes practicing not looking back at our past sins, failures, or achievements. This does not mean disregarding the learning experiences or the faith journey. It means that believers are to let go of the past and look to the future and the opportunities for growth in the present in their spiritual journey.

To Paul, the pursuit of spiritual excellence is a one-pointed effort on the goal that is set before him. This goal defines the heavenly prize that God has called him to in Christ Jesus. The primary aim of the apostle is to comprehend the will of God, to become like Christ, and to fulfill the purpose for which he has been called. It is a goal that goes beyond the material world and temporary success, reminding believers of the heavenly calling of their faith.

20

The Small Package

The Small Package

M y wise uncle shared many things with me during my youth. There is one quote that has stuck in my head for the past seventy-three years: "A man who is all wrapped up in himself makes for a small package." I can clearly recall the first time I heard that statement.

This quote perfectly describes the concept of narcissism and the consequences of the same for a person's personality and relationships with other people. It is a daily reminder to me to stay humble, kind, and receptive, as these qualities are important for a person's development and for building positive relationships with other people.

Ever since I have been alive, I have incorporated this quote in my life and have used it as a guide in my interactions with other people, making sure that I consider what other people need or want before what I need or want. This simple yet powerful quote has always motivated me to strive for self-improvement and growth.

The Bible also has several examples of people who had no empathy for others, no humility, and no concern for other people around them. For instance, the book of Proverbs tells the reader that it is better not to have friends than to have fools for friends. The description portrays these individuals as proud and self-important, always seeking personal gain and ignoring others' needs and feelings.

The book of James also has a lot to say about the subject of humility and the consequences of arrogance and boastfulness. Only the humble, those who are mindful of others' needs and experiences, find true wisdom. The Bible highlights empathy and humility as vital virtues crucial for strong relationships and a healthy society.

Today, America has become the opposite of what it used to be. This societal shift in values and beliefs is clear, even in our mainline churches. These churches that used to be very traditional in their thinking have now shifted their view to the world and have more progressive views on some issues. Instead of defending orthodox doctrines and principles, they now advocate for liberal and acceptable positions.

This shift is clear in how they advocate for same-sex marriage, gender identity, social justice, and equality. Secularism and popular culture have affected these churches, leading to a shift away from their original teachings and practices. This shift in American religion mirrors broader societal and individual changes.

In my hometown, one person stands out in my memory: Oliver. His preoccupation and solitary nature led people to label him a recluse. Oliver had a few friends. His small, cozy hut, filled with books, inventions, and his own thoughts, was where he spent most of his time.

So, I have a clear image of one cool autumn night when a storytelling woman by the name of Lettie came to our town. Her stories were famous for the ability to tell the audience the magic and wisdom of the world. She came walking up to a cookout we were having before a high school football game, and she began sharing her stories in the warmth of the communal bonfire. Oliver was there that night because the food was free!

While Oliver observed from a distance, Lettie began her tale. Her voice was mesmerizing, her stories eliciting laughter, tears, and a shared connection—that's what I remember about Lettie. Both Oliver and I were interested in one of her stories.

Miss Lettie recounted a tale about a wise elder. He told his people that self-centeredness is limiting, saying, "Self-absorbed people have little impact." I immediately remembered where I had first heard those words—my uncle.

Those words affected Oliver, leading him to recognize his self-imposed limitations. Motivated by the narrative, he ventured from his comfort zone and engaged with the townspeople. He shared his inventions, knowledge, and personal stories with the people.

Unexpectedly to Oliver, the townspeople welcomed him warmly. He brought in new light and views to the community. In return, he received friendship, comprehension, and a sense of belonging that he had never had before. The package he had once confined himself to expanded to a wide and multifaceted network of relationships and experiences.

We could see a change in the old recluse. A few years later, Oliver died, and the community came to the local funeral home to pay their last respects to him. That evening, my mom and I went to the funeral home and heard our townsfolk share how Oliver's life had changed. Oliver did not die alone.

I know a lot about the power of connection. In my 52 years of ministry, I have met many people, like Oliver, an old man in search of a place, and Miss Lettie, an old woman in search of company.

As a minister, I've also seen how insignificant gestures can change people. In the same way that Oliver found his place in our town, I have been lucky enough to experience the beauty of a person who will share themselves with others.

It is interesting to note that these insignificant gestures may result in forming wonderful friendships and dedicated support systems. These experiences have once again taught me the importance of connecting with people and building relationships, as they can really make a difference in our lives.

21

Clean Heart - Clean Home

Clean Heart - Clean Home

T he church, in its role as "cleaner," plays a significant role in society. Just as a cleaner meticulously tidys up a messy room, the church works to purify the souls of its members and promote moral righteousness. It serves as a guiding force, offering spiritual guidance and support to those seeking solace and direction in their lives. Through religious teachings, rituals, and practices, the church aims to cleanse individuals of their sins, encouraging them to lead virtuous lives.

The church acts as a moral compass, providing ethical frameworks and values that help shape the behavior and decisions of its followers. In this way, the church acts as a societal cleaner, working diligently to promote goodness, integrity, and spiritual well-being among its congregation.

The Bible offers many scriptures that exemplify the church in the role of cleaner. In the book of Ephesians, chapter 5, verse 26, it states, "That He might sanctify and cleanse it with the washing of water by the word." This verse emphasizes the church's role in purifying and cleansing its members through the teachings of the Word of God.

In 1 Corinthians 6:11, it is written, "And such were some of you: but ye are washed, but ye are sanctified, but ye are justified in the name of the Lord Jesus and by the Spirit of our God."

James 4:8 states, "Draw nigh to God, and He will draw nigh to you. Cleanse your hands, ye sinners; and purify your hearts, ye double-minded." This verse highlights the church's role in encouraging believers to constantly strive for spiritual cleanliness and purity. Overall, these scriptures depict the church as a place where individuals can find spiritual cleansing, redemption, and guidance in leading a righteous life.

The concept of a "church as a cleaner" often evokes the image of a sanctuary where individuals find solace, forgiveness, and a chance to start anew. Here are a few personal anecdotes from people who have experienced this firsthand:

Helen's Story: Helen had been battling addiction to drugs and alcohol for years. She felt trapped in a never-ending cycle of substance abuse and was losing hope of ever breaking free. One day, in a moment of desperation, she stumbled upon a local church during an open service. Intrigued, she walked in, not knowing what to expect. To her surprise, the congregation welcomed her with open arms, showing her kindness and acceptance she hadn't experienced in a long time. They didn't judge her for her struggles; instead, they offered her the help and support she so desperately needed. With the encouragement of the church community, Helen made the courageous decision to enter a rehab program. It was a challenging journey, but with the unwavering support of the church and her newfound faith, she could turn her life around. Helen is a shining example of strength and change. She volunteers at the same church, using her experience to help and inspire others who are going through similar struggles.

Mark's Transformation: Mark had made a series of poor decisions that resulted in him becoming estranged from his family. The weight of guilt and shame consumed him, leaving him feeling lost and alone. Searching for solace, he attended a service at a nearby church. Little did he know that this simple decision would be the turning point in his life. The pastor's sermon about forgiveness resonated deeply with Mark, stirring a desire within him to make amends and reconcile with his loved ones. Encouraged by the church community, he mustered the courage to reach out to his family and begin the long and challenging process of mending broken relationships. The church provided him with counseling and guidance throughout this journey, helping him navigate through the complexities of forgiveness and healing. Mark experienced a remarkable transformation as he embraced the love and support of the church, finding a sense of belonging that he had been missing for so long.

Lisa's New Beginning: Lisa had always been a strong and ambitious woman, but after unexpectedly losing her job, she sank into a deep state of anxiety and depression. The sudden loss of purpose left her feeling directionless and isolated from the world around her. In her darkest moments, a close friend reached out and invited her to attend a church service. Though hesitant at first, Lisa tried it. Little did she know that this simple act of stepping into a church would mark the beginning of a profound transformation. The church community welcomed her with open arms, providing a haven where she could share her struggles and find emotional support. Through various church activities, Lisa discovered new passions and a renewed sense of purpose. The love and encouragement she received from the church community empowered her to regain her confidence and embark on a journey of self-discovery. The church supported Lisa in finding a new job. Now a grateful and active member, she uses her experiences to inspire others.

These stories highlight how the church can serve as a "cleaner," offering people a chance to find hope, healing, and a fresh start in life.

Just as regular cleaning supplies clean our homes, Christ offers a cleansing of the heart. Romans 3:23 states that "For all have sinned and come short of the glory of God." This verse highlights the universal nature of sin, acknowledging that every individual, regardless of their background or circumstances, falls short of God's perfect standard. Sin, in its various forms, stains and pollutes our hearts, leaving us disconnected from God and in need of spiritual purification.

However, the good news is that Christ's sacrifice on the cross provides a solution to this problem. Through His death and resurrection, Jesus offers forgiveness for our sins and the opportunity to be reconciled with God. His love and grace can wash away the stains of sin, leaving our hearts cleansed and restored.

This spiritual cleansing goes beyond surface-level cleanliness; it penetrates deep into the core of our being, transforming us from the inside out. Just as cleaning supplies are essential for maintaining a clean and healthy home, Christ's forgiveness and redemption are crucial for our spiritual well-being.

By accepting His gift of salvation and allowing Him to cleanse our hearts, we can experience true freedom, joy, and a renewed relationship with our Heavenly Father.

22

History is a Science: Lessons of the Past and Future

❖

Throughout my childhood, I relied on my father's sage advice to help me whenever I made a mistake or did something wrong. Offering fatherly advice, he would gently tell me, in a comforting tone, "Live and learn, son," as if imparting wisdom from years of experience. In his view, every mistake, every stumble, every failure, however insignificant, served as a valuable lesson, contributing to his growing experience, strength, and overall stability.

Because of his teachings, I developed a positive attitude towards change, which enabled me to learn from my mistakes, grow from challenges, and become more resilient. Through his insightful guidance, I gained a profound understanding of how to navigate life's complexities with an open mind, a resilient spirit, and an unyielding curiosity for acquiring knowledge. My father's insightful words not only provided me with the support I needed to navigate this challenging period but also shaped my perspective on both the triumphs and setbacks inherent in the pursuit of success. With their help, I could view each event as a valuable opportunity for growth and learning, shaping my perspective and expanding my skill set.

We learn from experience, and experience includes both our failures and successes. The past, though gone, imparts valuable lessons and wisdom that we can and should apply to both our present circumstances and our future endeavors. Failures are outstanding teachers that show the mistakes that will probably to be made to be successful in a particular endeavor. They teach us resilience, determination, and the need to persist. Successes are inspiring and motivate us to keep on striving for greatness. They show the benefits of hard work, dedication, and decision making.

Both personal growth and professional development are essential for our advancement, contributing significantly to our overall well-being and helping us to evolve into better individuals in all aspects of our lives. Looking back, we can thus expect to glean valuable lessons from past mistakes, improving our ability to both effectively manage future challenges and fully seize emerging opportunities.

Understanding history involves comprehending the full spectrum of human actions, achievements, and failures as they have unfolded throughout the ages, a continuous cycle of progress and regress. Below, we outline some of history's most significant lessons.

The historical record shows that cooperation and a unified approach have been pivotal factors contributing to success at various points throughout the world's history. In the post-World War II era, the establishment of the United Nations stands out as a landmark achievement, representing a significant and unparalleled global effort to foster peace and facilitate the fair distribution of power among nations. When people work together, despite their differences, it is possible to achieve a tremendous deal, and this collaboration can foster a better and more peaceful world for all.

History shows that the fall of mighty empires, such as the Roman Empire, serves as a stark reminder of the perils of excessive self-assurance and the importance of humility in maintaining power. The overexpansion of their business, coupled with a feeling of complacency and a significant underestimation of the risks involved, led to their downfall. It is always necessary to exercise both modesty and caution in all that you do. It is of paramount importance to assess and continuously change the process, implementing changes as needed to maintain success.

The Industrial Revolution brought about sweeping changes to societies across the globe, altering economic structures and causing significant environmental impacts. Groundbreaking innovations in machinery, transportation, and communication systems were the driving forces behind the world's transition into the Industrial Age. While we must continue to pursue innovation, it is equally crucial that we carefully consider and mitigate the societal and environmental repercussions of technological advancements. Responsible innovation is critically important for the ethical and sustainable development of modern technologies and their applications.

This article reveals that the historical record is replete with inspiring narratives of individuals who valiantly championed justice, demonstrating courage and resilience in their pursuit of a fairer world. Noteworthy examples of impactful social change movements include, but are not limited to, the American Civil Rights Movement and the dismantling of the apartheid system in South Africa. Humans possess an indomitable spirit, a testament to our capacity to overcome adversity and persevere through even the most difficult circumstances. We pursue justice and societal transformation, significantly and meaningfully changing our communities.

The World Wars, both, are the examples of the catastrophic consequences of uncontrolled nationalism and aggression. It is important to learn from the past to prevent similar tragedies from happening in the future. Learning from past mistakes is essential for a successful future, and a study of history reveals invaluable lessons in effective diplomacy, conflict resolution strategies, and the crucial significance of fostering strong and positive relationships with other nations across the globe.

Mahatma Gandhi, Martin Luther King Jr., and Winston Churchill, all visionary leaders, each made significant and lasting contributions that have profoundly shaped the course of world history. The indelible mark left on society by their leadership styles and the decisions that resulted from them are undeniable and far-reaching. Through inspiration and motivation, it is possible to guide individuals toward making sound choices and performing commendable actions that contribute to the betterment of society. To cultivate effective leadership, it is crucial to foster and promote qualities such as empathy, a strong moral compass, and the ability to think strategically and make sound judgments.

As we move forward, it is of critical importance that we remember and apply the lessons of the past to guide our future decisions and actions. Through careful analysis of past events and trends, we possess the ability to craft a future that is not only more equitable and peaceful but also significantly more sustainable. History is far more than a mere accumulation of past occurrences; it is a complex tapestry woven from diverse experiences, social structures, and individual narratives that shape our present understanding. We have a responsibility to learn from history and to apply its lessons to our current challenges and circumstances in the modern world.

During my time serving as a pastor in a small town, a catastrophic hurricane devastated our community. The hurricane had a devastating impact on our region, resulting in widespread homelessness and leaving countless individuals without essential resources and necessities for survival. The aftermath of the disaster revealed an incredible outpouring of unity and cooperation between the churches and the community, a testament to their combined strength and resilience. Neighbors assisted one another with cleanup, local businesses made generous supply donations and provided temporary housing to the affected by various organizations. Through this experience, I learned the importance of unity and the strength that comes from people supporting each other during tough times, fostering a powerful sense of community and shared purpose.

During my college years as a young adult, I could witness firsthand the transformative effects of technological advancements on the educational environment. How students and I learned and accessed information underwent a significant transformation with introducing computers and the internet. This experience highlighted the transformative potential of technology in revolutionizing education and communication, while simultaneously raising serious concerns regarding its responsible and ethical application.

Back in my college days, a long, long time ago, the only computer available to the entire campus was a single, large room filled with fascinating and bulky computer equipment. Numerous large structures filled the room, their blinking lights creating a distinctly scientific atmosphere. Dominating the center of the room was a large screen and keyboard, an intriguing gateway to a completely different and exciting realm. Despite the three-hour drive to the prestigious University of Georgia in Athens, each student felt privileged to use and interact with the university's computer systems.

We accomplished this task by inputting messages into the mainframe and then patiently awaiting the responses, which were expected to be available the following day. In retrospect, I find it quite astonishing and beyond my imagination just how innovative and forward-thinking this technology was for us. The scene was so futuristic; it felt like a vision of the future. This future was far more advanced than our present.

In this modern era, it's impossible to envision a single day unfolding without the ubiquitous presence and integration of computers into every facet of our daily existence. From email correspondence and social networking to a vast array of other applications, computers have become indispensable tools used for everything we do. They have become so integrated into our lives that they are now indispensable, and we cannot live without them. I find it utterly incomprehensible how people coped with their daily lives before the invention of these items. I simply cannot fathom how they ever survived.

Reflecting on our journey, it's remarkable to see how far we've progressed and what we've achieved together. This clearly illustrates the significant advancements and positive changes in our community have implemented, displaying our progress. Technological advancements, social shifts, and evolving cultural norms have all contributed to an ongoing process of change and development throughout history. This phrase embodies the resilience of groups facing adversity, emphasizing their collective efforts and achievements. It speaks to overcoming impossible limits.

Our remarkable progress is a reminder of what we can achieve. It also inspires continued growth and development, both personally and socially. Reflecting on our past accomplishments, our gratitude fills us for the progress and growth we have achieved, and we eagerly expect the opportunities that lie ahead.

My grandmother, a remarkable woman, frequently shared detailed and vivid accounts of her life and her experiences of surviving the hardships of the Great Depression. Even though they faced extreme hardships, his family and he showed remarkable resilience and resourcefulness in overcoming them. In the challenging times, they relied on self-sufficiency, cultivating their own sustenance, crafting their own garments, and providing mutual support to help each other through.

In my grandmother's stories, she always emphasized the importance of their family's small backyard garden, where they grew an assortment of vegetables and fruits to feed their family. To ensure they had enough food to eat during the winter months, they would harvest all the produce from their gardens and carefully preserve it using various methods.

Her mother was remarkably skilled at sewing, mending, and transforming old clothes into new ones. She described this in her story. To get the things they could not cultivate themselves, they engaged in the practice of bartering with their immediate community, including both neighbors and friends. Although my grandmother's family lacked resources, they showed remarkable resilience, developing innovative strategies to ensure their survival and secure a livelihood.

Besides acquiring significant technical skills, I was most impressed by their exceptional teamwork and unwavering determination. During tough times, the tales of courage and optimism that I encountered instilled in me the resilience to remain strong and the persistent hopefulness to seek positivity even amidst adversity. There is a pattern in our history that causes this to happen repeatedly.

My mission trips exposed me to diverse cultures. I lived in their communities, learning about their lifestyles and perspectives. This transformative experience not only broadened my perspective and challenged my preconceived notions, but also significantly enriched my understanding of the complexities of the world. Besides its other effects, it also fostered cultural exchange and its many benefits from engaging with diverse perspectives. My son, live your life to the fullest and learn from every experience, both positive and negative, that comes your way.

The 21st century is fast paced, technologically advanced, globalized, and interconnected. Therefore, historical lessons are crucial. And to create a better future, it is beneficial to examine past events and learn from the mistakes and successes of the past. History is far more complex and nuanced than a simple recitation of dates and occurrences.

We can learn from history's triumphs and mistakes. By studying the past, we can strive for a more equitable and peaceful future, free from war and inequality.

Learning from history is crucial for cultivating empathy, compassion, and acceptance of others, as historical events teach us the importance of understanding diverse perspectives and experiences. This piece powerfully conveys the suffering caused by discrimination, prejudice, and hatred, while also inspiring the embrace of tolerance and equality. History illuminates the root causes of conflict, war, and injustice, thus paving the way for peaceful resolutions and preventing future atrocities. Throughout history, the power of collective action has repeatedly showed its ability to advance social justice, protect human rights, and strengthen democratic principles.

History provides not only moral guidance, but also offers practical knowledge and understanding, which are essential for navigating the complexities of life. Careful examination of the triumphs and shortcomings of diverse civilizations, societies, and economies throughout history achieves a comprehensive understanding of effective governance, sustainable development, and fair resource allocation. By studying historical trends and patterns, we can better identify potential problems and develop effective solutions for them. Therefore, by understanding both the errors and accomplishments of those who came before us, we can build upon their innovations, resulting in accelerated progress and enhanced stability.

Global challenges like climate change, inequality, poverty, and political instability are significant. We can learn from history to overcome them. This allows us to leverage the accumulated wisdom and experiences of countless generations, which helps us make better-informed decisions. Examining history helps us understand today's challenges. A just, peaceful, and environmentally sustainable future is likely if we learn from the past. History offers an invaluable treasure trove of knowledge, and it is of paramount importance that we diligently study its lessons and apply them to both contemporary and future difficulties.

23

Memorable Movie Moments

———⬦✦⬦———

Movies have a unique ability to transport us to different worlds, evoke powerful emotions, and leave us with lasting impressions. They often capture profound truths about the human experience, which can resonate deeply with the timeless wisdom found in scripture. In this article, we will explore some memorable movie moments from classic films that have left an indelible mark on our hearts and minds. From the heart-warming journey of self-discovery in "The Bucket List" to the inspiring tale of resilience and love in "Forrest Gump," these films have touched the lives of millions.

The thought-provoking themes of justice and compassion in "To Kill a Mockingbird" and the exhilarating pursuit of dreams in "The Walk" remind us of the values we hold dear. Finally, the poignant reflections on aging and family in "On Golden Pond" offer valuable insights into the complexities of life. By examining movie quotes and their scriptural references, we'll discover the films' deeper meaning and their inspirational power. This will deepen our appreciation of film.

I will begin with the movie "The Bucket List" starring Morgan Freeman and Jack Nicholson. In this heartwarming film, Morgan Freeman portrays the character of Carter Chambers and Jack Nicholson plays the role of Edward Cole. One memorable scene takes place atop an awe-inspiring

Egyptian pyramid, where Carter engages Edward in a thought-provoking conversation. Carter described the concept of the Egyptian Heaven, a mystical realm accessible only by answering two crucial questions posed by the guards at Heaven's entrance.

Intrigued, Edward implores Carter to share these profound questions with him. With a sense of anticipation in the air, Carter reveals the first question, "Have you found joy in your life?" This query prompts individuals to reflect on their own personal journey and assess happiness and fulfillment. Without pausing, Carter posed a second question: "Has your life brought joy to others?" This inquiry explores how one person's actions affect others, highlighting selflessness and positive impact. These two questions guide the movie. They also offer a profound message about life's purpose that resonates deeply with audiences.

In Carter's eulogy, Edward delivers a poignant statement that resonates deeply with the audience. He stresses the importance of a purposeful life. Our life will flash before our eyes one day, he says, when our journey ends. In that moment, we must have created a life story worthy of appreciation. It should be something to watch, savor, and treasure. This statement encourages us to live purposefully, making choices that reflect our values and goals, so we can positively affect the world.

Ephesians 5:15-16 is a passage from the Bible that provides guidance on how to live wisely and make the most of our time. The verse states, "See then that ye walk circumspectly, not as fools, but as wise, redeeming the time, because the days are evil." In this passage, the apostle Paul encourages believers to approach their lives with caution and wisdom. He urges them to be mindful of their actions and choices, avoiding foolishness and making wise decisions.

We must use our time and resources wisely, as the phrase "making the most of every opportunity" highlights, acknowledging that every day presents challenges and temptations. This passage serves as a reminder to live intentionally, seeking to make positive contributions and impact in the world. It encourages believers to seize every chance to do good, grow spiritually, and fulfill their purpose, all while being aware of the potential dangers and evils that may exist. Overall, Ephesians 5:15-16 calls for a mindful and purposeful approach to life, emphasizing the need to prioritize wisdom and discernment in all aspects of our daily existence.

The movie "Forrest Gump" introduces us to Forrest Gump, an endearing and simple-minded character played by Tom Hanks. Directed by Robert Zemeckis, this critically acclaimed film takes us on a journey through various decades of American history, seen through the eyes of Forrest. The story follows his life, from his childhood in Alabama, his time serving in the Vietnam War, to becoming a successful entrepreneur and a devoted friend.

Tom Hanks delivers a remarkable performance, portraying Forrest with a perfect blend of innocence, naivety, and genuine kindness. The film's narrative structure cleverly weaves together historical events and personal anecdotes, creating a captivating and heartwarming tale. With its iconic quotes, such as "Life is like a box of chocolates," Forrest Gump has become a cultural phenomenon and continues to be adored by audiences worldwide.

One of my favorite moments from the movie is when Forrest, the main character played by Tom Hanks, delivers a memorable line. In this scene, Forrest is sitting on a park bench, recounting his life story to strangers. With his signature simplicity and innocence, Forrest utters a profound piece of advice that has resonated with audiences worldwide. He says, "My mama always said, 'You've got to put the past behind you before you can move on.'" These words encapsulate Forrest's unwavering optimism and his ability to overcome the obstacles life throws at him. They highlight the importance of letting go of experiences and focusing on the present moment to forge a better future. This quote has become an iconic part of the film, exemplifying Forrest's wisdom and touching the hearts of viewers with its universal message of resilience and hope.

Isaiah 43:18-19 is a passage from the Old Testament of the Bible that contains a message of hope and renewal. In these verses, the prophet Isaiah addresses the people of Israel, urging them to forget the past and look forward to the future. He encourages them not to dwell on the former things, which may include past mistakes, failures, or even victories.

Instead, Isaiah declares God is about to do something new and extraordinary in their lives. He promises God will make a way in the wilderness and create rivers in the desert. This powerful imagery conveys the idea that God can bring forth new life and transformation, even in the most challenging and barren situations. Through these words, Isaiah offers reassurance to the Israelites that God is with them and will guide them through any difficulties they may face. Believers today still find encouragement and inspiration in this passage. It reminds them to trust in God's power to renew and bring hope.

One of my all-time favorite movies is "To Kill a Mockingbird," a cinematic masterpiece that captivates audiences with its poignant storytelling and thought-provoking themes. The film, adapted from Harper Lee's classic novel, transports viewers to the fictional town of Maycomb, Alabama, in the 1930s, where racial injustice and moral dilemmas take center stage. Miss Maudie, a wise and compassionate character, beautifully encapsulates the essence of the movie when she states, "Mockingbirds don't do one thing but make music for us to enjoy. They don't eat up people's gardens, don't nest in corncribs, they don't do one thing but sing their hearts out for us. That's why it's a sin To Kill a Mockingbird."

Matthew 10:31 is a verse from the Bible in which Jesus delivers a message of reassurance and encouragement to his disciples. In this passage, Jesus tells his followers not to be afraid, emphasizing their inherent worth and value. He compares them to sparrows, a common bird stating that they are worth more than many sparrows.

This statement highlights the significance and worthiness of everyone, reminding them God cherished and loved them. Jesus' words serve as a reminder to his disciples, and to all believers, that they should not let fear or doubt diminish their sense of self-worth and purpose.

"To Kill a Mockingbird" explores the timeless themes of innocence, justice, and the destructive power of prejudice. Scout Finch, a young girl, and her lawyer father, Atticus Finch, are central to the story. It takes place in a racially divided society, where Atticus defends a wrongly accused Black man. The narrative unfolds through Scout's eyes, providing a unique perspective on the complex issues faced by Maycomb's residents.

Lee's novel, and subsequently the film, delves deep into the notion of innocence and its vulnerability in the face of bigotry. Scout, along with her brother Jem and friend Dill, experiences a loss of innocence as they witness the unjust treatment of Tom Robinson, the man Atticus defends. Through their interactions with Boo Radley, a reclusive neighbor, the children learn empathy and the importance of challenging societal norms.

"To Kill a Mockingbird" highlights the destructive power of prejudice and the damaging effects it has on individuals and communities. The film confronts the deeply ingrained racism prevalent in Maycomb, challenging viewers to confront their own biases and prejudices. By humanizing the marginalized and shedding light on the consequences of discrimination, the movie urges audiences to reevaluate their own beliefs and strive for a more inclusive society. According to Miss Maudie, the mockingbird's song embodies innocence and beauty deserving protection; therefore, destroying it is a sin.

"The Walk" is a movie about the incredible true story of high-wire artist Philippe Petit's daring and death-defying walk between the Twin Towers of the World Trade Center in 1974. Directed by Robert Zemeckis, this gripping biographical drama displays Petit's meticulous planning, his audacious dream, and the extraordinary feat of balancing on a wire suspended 1,350 feet above the ground.

The film examines Petit's preparations for his clandestine walk. These included team assembly, undetected tower access, and high-wire setup coordination. Through stunning visuals and heart-stopping moments, "The Walk" captures the sheer courage and determination of a man who defied all odds to achieve the impossible.

In a moving moment, Philippe Petit, a French high-wire artist, aerialist, and daredevil, expresses a profound sentiment about the power of dreams. He states, "Every dreamer knows it is entirely possible to be homesick for a place you've never been to, perhaps more homesick than for familiar ground."

Petit's words encapsulate the extraordinary connection between dreams and the longing for an unknown destination. It highlights the innate human desire to seek new experiences and uncharted territories, even if they exist solely in the realm of imagination. This sentiment speaks to those with a deep longing for adventure and discovery. They believe the world holds limitless possibilities beyond their comfort zone. Petit's words remind us that not only the comfort of the known drives the human spirit, but also the magnetic pull of what could be.

1 Corinthians 1:25 is a Bible verse that states, "Because the foolishness of God is wiser than men, and the weakness of God is stronger than men." The apostle Paul wrote this verse. In this passage, Paul is addressing the Corinthians, emphasizing the contrast between divine wisdom and human wisdom, as well as the power of God compared to human strength.

He highlights that even the perceived foolishness and weakness of God surpasses the wisdom and strength of human beings. This verse serves as a reminder of the superiority of God's ways and the importance of relying on His wisdom and strength rather than solely on human understanding.

In my search for a captivating and thought-provoking movie, my last offer is the timeless classic, "On Golden Pond." This heartfelt film stars the iconic Katherine Hepburn, who portrays the character of Ethel Thayer. Ethel's poignant line, "We're all just passing through," serves as a powerful reflection on the transient nature of life and the profound emotions that accompany it.

"On Golden Pond" is a cinematic masterpiece that explores the complexities of aging, family dynamics, and the beauty of human connections. A beloved lakeside cottage on Golden Pond serves as the setting for the film. Ethel and her husband Norman (Henry Fonda) spend their summer there. Their estranged daughter Chelsea, her fiancé Bill, and Bill's son Billy disrupted their tranquil existence.

Katherine Hepburn's portrayal of Ethel Thayer is nothing short of extraordinary. Ethel is a vibrant and spirited woman who possesses unwavering love and devotion for her husband, Norman. Despite the inevitable challenges that come with aging, Ethel remains a source of strength and wisdom throughout the film. Her line, "We're all just passing through," encapsulates her profound understanding of the fleeting nature of life and the importance of cherishing every moment.

Beyond its captivating storyline and exceptional performances, "On Golden Pond" conveys a universal message that resonates with audiences of all ages. Ethel's words serve as a reminder to embrace the impermanence of life, urging us to live fully and appreciate the beauty that surrounds us. The film prompts introspection and encourages viewers to reevaluate their relationships and priorities, inspiring them to cherish their loved ones and make the most of every fleeting moment.

I Peter 1:24 states, "For all flesh is as grass, and all the glory of man as the flower of grass. The grass withereth, and the flower thereof falleth away." This verse, found in the New Testament of the Bible, is part of a letter written by the apostle Peter to the early Christian believers. In this passage, Peter uses a simile to convey the fleeting nature of human existence and the temporary nature of worldly achievements. He compares people to grass, emphasizing their fragility and transience. Just as grass withers and flowers eventually fade and fall, so too does human life and all its earthly glory. This verse reminds us that eternal values and faith are more important than worldly things. Focus on what lasts, not what's temporary.

Now perhaps you can recall some epic films you've watched and how they've affected your life. Compare quotes from the movies and relate them scripturally. There are always "diamonds in the rough" to be gleamed.

24

The Unexpected Gift of a Clean Billfold

In the realm of forgetfulness, I have earned quite the reputation for my uncanny ability to leave various objects nestled within the depths of my pants pockets. Alas, this innocent habit has aroused the annoyance of my dear wife, who endures the additional work it entails during laundry day. Despite my best efforts to explain away my absentmindedness, my attempts at justification have proven futile in appeasing her exasperation.

From an early age, my propensity for absentmindedness has been a defining characteristic of my existence. Although I possess an astute memory for certain matters, my pants pockets have become a black hole for many items. Whether it be stray receipts, spare change, or even the occasional pen, these precious belongings find solace in the hidden recesses of my trousers, much to my wife's chagrin.

My forgetful nature may be a funny story for family get-togethers, but it affects my wife's daily routine. As she gathers the clothes for a much-needed wash, her hands stumble upon these hidden treasures, resulting in her having to inspect each pocket. This unexpected chore not only adds extra time and effort to her already busy schedule but also introduces an element of frustration that threatens to overshadow our domestic bliss.

I have attempted to provide explanations for my forgetfulness, knowing full well the gravity of my actions. However, my excuses, no matter how creative or plausible, often fall short of convincing my wife. Whether it be blaming a hectic day at work, the distractions of modern life, or even the mysterious force of gravity, none of these justifications seem to ease her frustration. Therefore, I acknowledge she sees my excuses, however well-intentioned, as weak attempts to avoid responsibility.

In the realm of domestic harmony, the forgotten treasures of my pants pockets have proven to be a point of contention between my wife and me. I shoulder the burden of my forgetfulness, but I must recognize its effect on others. With newfound determination, I vow to remember the contents of my pockets, sparing my wife the unnecessary hassle and ensuring a smoother journey through the ever-present chore of laundry day.

My wife surprised me by returning my billfold that she had found after washing it in my pants. To my amazement, the billfold gleamed for the first time since I bought it. As I opened it, I couldn't help but notice that everything inside was in pristine condition - my credit cards, money, and even my driver's license.

However, nestled deep inside one pocket, I discovered a small, folded piece of paper that the washing machine had soaked. I unfolded the paper to find the name of a long-lost friend written on it. Memories flooded back as I remembered meeting his wife at a restaurant years ago. She told me about his heartbreaking battle with Alzheimer's. She asked if I could contact him and cheer him up. I intended to assure her I would make that call, but somehow, I forgot about the little folded piece of paper tucked away in my billfold all this time.

I carefully arranged the wet papers so they could dry, and then I took some time to call up my old friend, catching up on some long-awaited news. Initially, he failed to recognize my voice; however, upon my revealing my identity, he understood. "Well, well, well, if it isn't Charles Cravey!

What in the world? It has been so many years since I last saw you. I honestly thought you had died years ago." My friend said with a chuckle.

I told him I was still alive. He is now up to date on recent events, thanks to me. I also explained that I'd met his wife at a restaurant, and she'd given me his number. He finally said, in a broken voice, "Thank you for calling me, Charles. I needed to hear a voice from my past, for I stay confused most of the time. Let's stay in touch."

I promised my friend that I would call again later in the week. He had been going through a challenging time and had expressed his gratitude for our previous conversation. During that call, he had confided in me about his struggles and described my call as a soothing balm for his weary soul. Hearing my words brought him comfort and relief. After expressing my appreciation for his kind words, we exchanged our goodbyes and ended the call on a positive note.

Ecclesiastes 4:9-10 (NIV): "Two are better than one, because they have a good reward for their labour: For if they all, the one will lift up his fellow: but woe to him that is alone when he falleth; for he hath not another to help him up."

There was a time when I struggled with a personal issue that weighed heavily on my heart. One evening, while out on a walk to clear my mind, I wandered into a quaint little chapel. I sat down and allowed the serenity of the place to envelop me. As I sat in silence, a sense of peace and clarity washed over me, as if guided by a higher power. That experience reminded me that sometimes, spiritual guidance and solace can be found in the most unexpected places.

Sometimes we all need a thorough cleansing of our hearts, souls, and minds. We should also regularly cleanse ourselves spiritually.

Psalm 51:10 (NIV): "Create in me a clean heart, O God; and renew a right spirit within me."

2 Corinthians 5:17 (NIV): "Therefore, if any man be in Christ, he is a new creature: old things are passed away; behold, all things are become new."

In Psalm 51:10, David is expressing his plea for a clean heart and renewed spirit. This verse is a part of David's prayer of repentance after the prophet Nathan confronted him for his adulterous affair with Bathsheba and the murder of her husband, Uriah. David acknowledges his transgressions and asks God to create in him a pure heart and to renew a steadfast spirit within him. This verse shows David's desire for forgiveness and restoration as he seeks to abandon his sinful ways and reconcile with God.

In 2 Corinthians 5:17, Paul is referring to the transformative power of Christ's salvation. He states, "Therefore, if anyone is in Christ, the new creation has come: The old has gone, the new is here!" Here, Paul is emphasizing that when people accept Jesus Christ as their Savior, they experience a complete spiritual rebirth. This transformation is not just a superficial change, but a profound shift in their identity and nature. Paul emphasizes Christ's redemptive work's incredible impact on believers' lives, freeing them from sin's bondage and giving them a fresh start. This verse serves as a reminder of the radical change that occurs when someone becomes a follower of Christ and the hope that comes from being made new in Him.

In the journey of life, there are moments that have the power to cleanse our hearts, bringing forth a sense of renewal and rejuvenation. These moments can arise unexpectedly, catching us off guard, but their impact is profound. This article explores three such experiences that contribute to the cleansing of our hearts: an unexpected call from an old friend, a billfold cleansing, and an act of forgiveness.

1. An Unexpected Call from an Old Friend:

Sometimes, amidst the chaos of our daily lives, we receive an unexpected call from someone we haven't heard from in years - an old friend. The mere sound of his/her voice sparks a surge of emotions and memories, instantly transporting us back to cherished moments shared. This unexpected connection serves as a reminder of the bond we once had and the depth of the relationships we form throughout our lives. The conversation that ensues becomes a cleansing force, washing away any bitterness or distance that may have crept into our hearts. It rekindles a sense of connection and reminds us of the importance of nurturing and valuing the relationships that truly matter.

2. Billfold Cleansing:

In the hustle and bustle of our materialistic world, we often accumulate unnecessary clutter, both physically and emotionally. Our billfolds, filled with old receipts, expired cards, and forgotten scraps, become a metaphorical representation of this clutter. Organizing and cleaning our wallets can be a therapeutic and cathartic experience, benefiting both our financial well-being and emotional state. Sorting through the remnants of our past purchases and discarding what no longer serves a purpose can be a liberating experience. It helps us let go of attachments to material possessions and invites a sense of simplicity and clarity into our lives. This act of billfold cleansing has the power to cleanse our hearts, freeing us from the burdens of excess and reminding us of the importance of mindful consumption.

3. Acts of Forgiveness:

One of the most transformative experiences that can cleanse our hearts is the act of forgiveness. Holding onto grudges and harboring resentment only weighs us down, preventing us from experiencing true peace and happiness. However, when we choose to forgive, we liberate ourselves from the shackles of anger and bitterness. Forgiveness is not about condoning or forgetting the hurt caused; rather, it is a conscious decision to let go of negative emotions and move forward with a lighter heart. By extending forgiveness, we create space within ourselves for healing, compassion, and growth. It is a powerful act that not only cleanses our hearts but also fosters deeper connections with others and promotes a more harmonious existence.

The cleansing of our hearts is a continuous journey, filled with unexpected moments and transformative experiences. An unexpected call from an old friend, a billfold cleansing, and acts of forgiveness are just a few examples of the countless opportunities we encounter along the way. These moments remind us of the importance of nurturing relationships, letting go of material attachments, and embracing forgiveness. As we engage in these cleansing experiences, we pave the way for a more peaceful, joyful, and fulfilled life.

The cleansed life is a happy life. Is there someone you need to call today from your past? Is there something in your life that needs a cleansing? Do you need forgiveness and a fresh start? Then begin today with Jesus. Go to the cross and you'll find that cleansing power that will wash away your sins and set you free.

25

Nostalgia and Faith

---❖---

I once had a mentor who would often share stories of his own faith journey, reflecting on how God had guided him through various challenges. His nostalgic reflections were not just stories of the past, but lessons that illuminated the path forward. His experiences reassured me that, no matter what, God's guidance is steadfast and ever-present. He would often mention the Israelites in the wilderness and how they longed for earlier days under captivity in Egypt.

Numbers 11:5-6 reveals that, while journeying through the wilderness, the Israelites yearned for the food they had enjoyed in Egypt. They fondly reminisced about the varied and flavorful meals they had partaken in Egypt, including fish, cucumbers, melons, leeks, onions, and garlic. That they received these delicacies at no cost made these memories particularly alluring. In stark contrast, the Israelites now found themselves sustained solely by the manna, a miraculous bread-like substance that appeared every morning on the ground. They expressed their discontent, lamenting that their appetite had waned because of the monotonous nature of their daily sustenance. They longed for the diversity and abundance they had experienced before, unable to appreciate the unique provision of the manna in their current circumstances. This passage highlights the human tendency to pine for the past and overlook the blessings of the present.

During my childhood, Sunday mornings were always a special time for me. As a child, I would eagerly wake up to the sound of hymns being sung by the congregation, filling our small church with beautiful melodies. The smell of freshly polished pews and the comforting warmth of the surrounding people created an atmosphere that felt like home. Those Sunday mornings were more than just a religious obligation; they were a time for our community to come together and strengthen our faith.

The church I attended was a Pentecostal church known for its lively worship services. As soon as the music started, parishioners would rise to their feet, singing and shouting praises to God. It was a remarkable sight, with people joyfully running up and down the aisles, fully embracing the Holy Spirit. These worship services were unlike anything I had ever experienced before, and they left an impression on my young soul.

One thing I loved most about our church was the passionate preaching. Our pastor was not a scholarly theologian, but a charismatic speaker who delivered fiery "fire and brimstone" sermons. He had a way of engaging the congregation and delivering messages that inspired and challenged us. Some find this preaching style intimidating; it powerfully reminded me of the consequences of actions and the importance of righteousness.

Looking back on those days, I can't help but feel a sense of nostalgia. That Pentecostal church filled Sunday mornings with energy, devotion, and a genuine sense of community. It was a place where I felt loved, supported, and encouraged in my faith. Attending a church service now instantly transports me back to those cherished memories, reminding me of the foundations of my faith and the power of a close-knit community.

Yesterday will always be nostalgic for us, regardless of what happened then. It was a day filled with a mix of emotions and memories that have left an indelible mark on our hearts. Sunrise to sunset, each moment felt special. The day began with a golden glow and ended in vibrant orange and pink hues. It was the laughter shared with loved ones, the tears shed during moments of vulnerability, or the unexpected surprises that made the day truly unforgettable.

Whatever the case may be, yesterday will forever hold a special place in our hearts as a time when life felt alive and vibrant. The sights, sounds, and scents of that day remain imprinted on our minds, instantly transporting us back to a time when everything felt perfect. Even if we faced challenges and overcame obstacles, the thought of yesterday brings comfort and a flood of cherished memories. Remember: Yesterday's beauty and joy will always bring solace, no matter what the future holds.

One early church father, Augustine of Hippo (354-430 AD), gave us his profound theological contributions about nostalgia. His writings, particularly his renowned work "Confessions," delve into various themes, with a special emphasis on memory and the human yearning for God. Augustine intricately intertwined his understanding of nostalgia with the concept of longing for the divine. In "Confessions," he intimately reflects upon his past transgressions and the boundless mercy bestowed upon him by God. Through his introspection, Augustine expresses a profound desire to return to a state of grace and communion with the divine. Augustine wrote, "You created us for yourself, O Lord; and our hearts are restless until they find rest in you."

Another early church father was Gregory of Nyssa (335-395 AD). Gregory, a prominent figure in early Christianity, made significant contributions to Christian mysticism and theology. His writings frequently explore the concept of the soul's journey back to God, focusing on the profound longing for the divine presence that permeates the human experience.

This spiritual nostalgia serves as a powerful driving force, propelling the soul's relentless ascent towards God. Gregory's central idea, known as "epektasis," underscores the notion that the soul is in a constant state of progression, ceaselessly moving closer to its divine origin. This concept highlights the perpetual yearning to return to its true home in God, shaping the spiritual path of believers who seek ultimate union with the divine. Gregory's profound insights and teachings continue to inspire and guide Christians on their spiritual journeys today.

A modern-day church father was C.S. Lewis (1898-1963). Lewis, a modern Christian apologist and author, explored themes of longing and nostalgia in his works. He was a prominent figure in the mid-20th century, known for his insightful writings on Christianity and the human experience.

Lewis delved into the depths of human longing and nostalgia, seeking to understand the universal yearning for something more, something beyond the confines of this earthly existence. In his essay "The Weight of Glory," Lewis delves into the concept of sehnsucht, a German word that encompasses a deep, intrinsic longing for a heavenly home. This profound yearning, according to Lewis, is spiritual nostalgia, reflecting a desire for a transcendent reality beyond the limitations of our current world.

Through his words, Lewis invites readers to ponder the essence of this longing and to contemplate the significance of yearning for something beyond what we can see and touch. "The scent of a flower we have not found, the echo of a tune we have not heard, news from a country we have never yet visited." This poignant quote captures the essence of a deep, spiritual nostalgia that Lewis sought to convey throughout his writings. It speaks to the longing within every human heart for a reality that surpasses our current experience, hinting at the existence of a greater, more fulfilling existence awaiting us. C.S. Lewis, through his exploration of nostalgia and longing, invites readers to embrace this sehnsucht and to seek a deeper understanding of their own spiritual journey.

Another modern-day church father was Henri Nouwen (1932-1996).

Henri Nouwen was a highly influential figure in the realm of Catholic spirituality. As a Catholic priest and theologian, he dedicated his life to exploring and understanding the intricacies of spiritual life and pastoral care. Nouwen's writings, which span a wide range of topics, delve deep into the human longing for intimacy with God and how individuals can cultivate a meaningful relationship with the divine.

One of the central themes that emerges from Nouwen's writings is the concept of nostalgia. Nouwen eloquently describes the innate human longing for intimate connection with God, a profound sense of belonging, and wholeness. Nouwen believes that this longing for connection stems from a deep-seated nostalgia for the perfect union with God that humanity once had and lost. Through his writings, Nouwen seeks to guide individuals on a path toward rediscovering this lost connection and finding solace and fulfillment in God's love and grace.

In his renowned work, "The Return of the Prodigal Son," Nouwen brilliantly uses the parable as a metaphor for the soul's journey back to the loving embrace of God. Drawing inspiration from Rembrandt's painting of the same name, Nouwen explores the themes of forgiveness, reconciliation, and redemption. He skillfully weaves together his own individual experiences, reflections, and theological insights to offer readers a profound and transformative understanding of the parable. Through this exploration, Nouwen invites individuals to embark on their own spiritual journey, evoking a sense of longing and nostalgia for a deep and meaningful relationship with God.

As we reflect on past blessings, we remember our heritage, our hopes, and our dreams. In today's challenging times, these sources of comfort and resilience help us endure even the most troubling situations.

In Psalm 77:11-12, the psalmist expresses a deep desire to remember and reflect on the deeds of the Lord. The psalmist acknowledges the miracles that God has performed in the past and makes a deliberate choice to meditate on the mighty works of God. This passage highlights the importance of recalling and contemplating the blessings and miracles that God has given.

Nostalgia, often associated with a longing for the past, can have a positive impact on our faith and trust in God. Remembering the miracles of long ago can serve as a source of encouragement and reassurance in times of uncertainty. Reflecting on God's mighty deeds reminds us of his faithfulness and power, strengthening our confidence in his ability to work in our lives today.

Amid challenges and difficulties, it is easy to lose sight of the blessings we have received. However, intentionally considering all of God's works helps us regain perspective and appreciate the goodness poured out upon us. Taking the time to meditate on the miracles of the past allows us to connect with God on a deeper level and cultivate a grateful heart.

Therefore, as we journey through life, let us remember the deeds of the Lord and recall His miracles of long ago. May we continually consider all His works and meditate on His mighty deeds, for it is through reflection on these blessings that we can find strength, hope, and renewed faith in God.

26

Peanuts, Faith, and a President

My dear friend Hank, a traveling sales agent, came to spend the night with my wife and me before traveling to another town the following morning. He had a special request: would I please take him to Plains, Georgia, to hear Jimmy Carter's farewell speech that evening before the election returns? We were only about an hour's drive away from Plains, so I agreed to take him, although I thought he was crazy to imagine Carter ever being elected President. After all, Carter was a peanut farmer from deep southwest Georgia, and it seemed like he had nothing in common with the political world of Washington. But Hank was determined, and I couldn't resist his enthusiasm.

Upon arrival in Plains, we found hundreds of people gathered around the train depot, eagerly expecting Carter's speech before departing for Atlanta to hear the election results later in the evening. Hank, who is small in stature, requested to climb on my shoulders for a better view of Carter and to snap some pictures of him in the crowd. Without hesitation, I agreed to let him climb up. The atmosphere was electric as Carter began his farewell speech. His calmness and sincerity shone through, captivating the crowd. We watched in awe as he finished his speech and got into the car that would take him to Atlanta.

That night, back at home, Hank insisted on watching the election results unfold. I was more interested in catching up on my favorite sitcom, Three's Company. But Hank's excitement and determination won the day, and we settled in to watch the results.

"Charles, turn the TV over to Channel 10, Albany, and let's see the election returns. I just know that Carter's going to win!" Hank declared excitedly, his anticipation of the election results palpable. With the country on the edge of its seat, he couldn't bear to miss a single moment of this historic event.

However, I felt a wave of indifference wash over me. "Hank, there is no way I'm going to sit here and watch those boring election returns!" I stated firmly, my disinterest clear in my tone. As the TV screen flickered to life, displaying the familiar news anchor preparing to announce the latest developments, I couldn't help but wonder if my apathy towards politics a missed opportunity was to engage in an important civic duty.

As the night wore on and the last results trickled in, Carter had emerged victorious. We stayed up well past midnight, celebrating the unexpected victory of our candidate. It was a momentous night, one that I would never forget.

And that was just the beginning. Carter became, to me, the best president possible. His charm, southern ways, and faith, put him at the top of my list. His career, after four good years, saw him become an avid worker with Habitat for Humanity, helping to build homes for the less advantaged. He began peace talks and mission work in various African nations. Carter's dedication to humanitarian efforts and his commitment to promoting peace and equality globally solidified his status as a remarkable leader. Besides his post-presidential activities, Carter also authored several books, sharing his wisdom and experiences with the world. His contributions to society extended beyond his time in office, making him a beloved figure both nationally and internationally.

Tonight, I watched the funeral service from the Washington National Cathedral, and I was so full of pride and thankfulness for the role this peanut farmer played. The funeral service honored a man who will forever be remembered for his unwavering faith in God. The Washington National Cathedral, a symbol of American history and spirituality, provided a fitting backdrop for honoring the life and legacy of this remarkable individual. Reflecting on the eulogies and his life's journey, the immense impact he had on our nation and the world struck me, leaving me in awe.

Through his humble beginnings as a peanut farmer in Georgia, he rose to become the 39th President of the United States, serving with integrity and a deep sense of purpose. Beyond his political achievements, it was his unwavering faith that truly stood out. Throughout his life, he consistently relied on his relationship with God to guide his decisions and actions. This steadfast devotion to his faith resonated with people from all levels of society, regardless of their religious beliefs.

Tonight, as I watched the funeral service, I thought of the profound influence one person can have if he lives his life under deeply held beliefs. This peanut farmer turned president touched the hearts and minds of millions, leaving behind a legacy of compassion, justice, and unwavering faith.

People recognized Jimmy Carter for more than just his political career; they also admired his strong moral compass. Throughout his life, he consistently adhered to the principles outlined in Micah 6:8. This verse from the Bible states, "He has shown you, O mortal, what is good. And what does the Lord require of you? To act justly and to love mercy and to walk humbly with your God."

In his pursuit of justice, Carter promoted human rights, both domestically and internationally. During his presidency, he fought for the equal rights of women and minorities and worked towards the improvement of living conditions for marginalized communities. Beyond his political tenure, he continued to advocate for justice by establishing the Carter Center, an organization dedicated to promoting peace, democracy, and human rights worldwide.

Carter's commitment to loving mercy was clear in his compassionate approach towards those in need. He emphasized the importance of empathy and kindness and engaged in humanitarian efforts. Through his work with Habitat for Humanity, he helped build homes for low-income families, demonstrating his belief in the power of generosity and compassion.

Despite his achievements and influence, Carter remained humble throughout his life. He approached his responsibilities with a sense of humility, recognizing the limitations of his own knowledge and abilities. This humility allowed him to listen to different perspectives, seek counsel, and make informed decisions for the betterment of society.

Jimmy Carter's life and actions exemplified the principles outlined in Micah 6:8. He acted justly, loved mercy, and walked humbly with his God. His commitment to justice, compassion, and humility left a lasting impact on the world and serves as an inspiration for generations to come.

Let me reiterate those three traits of a true Christian before closing. To act justly means to exhibit fairness, equity, and righteousness in our actions and dealings with others. It involves treating all individuals with respect and dignity, regardless of their background, social status, or beliefs. Acting justly entails standing up against injustice, oppression, and discrimination, and working towards creating a more fair and inclusive society. Advocating for the rights and well-being of the marginalized and vulnerable involves addressing systemic issues, perpetuating inequality, and aiming for a world with equal opportunities and resource access.

In our personal relationships, acting justly requires treating others with kindness, empathy, and compassion, and valuing their inherent worth as fellow human beings. Ultimately, acting justly as a true Christian aligns with the teachings of Jesus Christ, who emphasized the importance of loving our neighbors as ourselves and seeking justice for all.

Next, a true Christian loves mercy. Jesus Christ's teachings highlight mercy as a fundamental virtue. It is not just about feeling pity or compassion for others, but also about actively showing kindness and forgiveness. A true Christian understands the importance of extending mercy to others, recognizing that they, too, are imperfect and in need of grace.

Believers root their love for mercy in the belief that God is merciful and has shown great mercy towards humanity by sending His Son to die for their sins. A true Christian seeks to emulate this divine mercy in their interactions with others, seeking opportunities to forgive, show compassion, and help those in need. They understand that mercy is not only a demonstration of God's love, but also a way to bring healing and reconciliation to broken relationships and communities. Therefore, a true Christian's love for mercy is not just a passive sentiment, but an active practice that reflects his or her faith and commitment to following the example of Christ.

Last, walking humbly with God is a fundamental aspect of a person's spiritual journey. It involves acknowledging one's own limitations and weaknesses while recognizing God's sovereignty and guidance. Walking humbly with God requires a posture of humility, where individuals submit themselves to God's will and seek His wisdom in all aspects of life. This includes cultivating a spirit of gratitude, acknowledging God's blessings, and seeking His forgiveness when one falls short.

Walking humbly with God also involves developing a deep and intimate relationship with Him through prayer, meditation, and studying His Word. It is a continuous process of surrendering one's own desires and aligning oneself with God's purpose for their life. Through this humble walk, individuals can experience spiritual growth, find peace, and live a life that is pleasing to God.

There you have it. Those three aspects of a well-lived Christian lifestyle make for a great three-point sermon in any pulpit!

I will always cherish the memories of that unforgettable afternoon in Plains, Georgia, when my dear friend Hank and I witnessed an extraordinary moment in history. As we stood side by side, I could feel the excitement and anticipation building in the air. The sun shone brightly overhead, casting a warm glow on the crowd gathered before us. Hank, with his infectious laughter and boundless enthusiasm, sat comfortably on my shoulders, his eyes sparkling with anticipation. We did not know that we would remember this day forever. Initially, Carter had no chance at all becoming our 39th President, but it turned out I was completely wrong. The magnitude of God's intellect exceeds all my previous conceptions, leaving me in awe.

Unfortunately, Hank's health deteriorated, and he departed this world too soon, causing a void that can never be filled. As fate would have it, former President Jimmy Carter celebrated his 100th birthday just a few months ago. This incredible milestone touched the hearts of millions worldwide. And now, reunited in the realms of heaven, Hank and President Carter can finally meet face to face. Hank must feel immense joy as he shakes hands with his lifelong hero, a man who inspired him with dedication to public service and compassion. Together, they will forever watch over us, their spirits intertwined in the tapestry of history, reminding us that heroes never truly leave us.

27

The Revelation of Home

❦

In *The Midnight Library (p. 284) Penguin Books*, Matt Haig states, "It is quite a revelation to discover that the place you wanted to escape to is the exact same place you escaped from." This profoundly resonates with the parable of the prodigal son found in Luke 15:11-32. This narrative offers rich insights into human longing, self-discovery, and the transformative power of returning to one's roots—both physically and spiritually. The parable depicts a younger son asking for his inheritance and leaving for a distant country, believing he will find freedom and fulfillment there. However, after squandering all his wealth and experiencing the harsh realities of life, he realizes that his true home and sense of belonging lie in the loving embrace of his father.

This realization powerfully reminds us that what we seek outside ourselves is already within, and that we find true fulfillment only by embracing our authentic selves and reconnecting with our roots. Just as the prodigal son returns to his father and experiences forgiveness and restoration, we, too, can find redemption and transformation by returning to the essence of who we are and embracing the love and acceptance that awaits us. In this way, Haig's quote, and the parable of the prodigal son both highlight the profound truth that the very place we long to escape from may hold the keys to our ultimate happiness and fulfillment.

1. The Journey of the Prodigal Son

Haig's quote, "... the place you wanted to escape to is the exact same place you escaped from," resonates deeply with the son's epiphany. Throughout his journey, he gradually comes to realize the ironic truth that the very place he had yearned to escape from is the same place he longs to return to. This realization emphasizes the cyclical nature of his experiences and the inherent futility of seeking fulfillment and purpose in external locations. Initially driven by a fervent desire to break free from his mundane surroundings, the son embarks on a quest for something more meaningful elsewhere. However, he slowly realizes that his search for answers will be fruitless in the external world, as he encounters unusual places and people. Instead, one can only discover true meaning within oneself and one's familiar surroundings, the very ones he once wanted to leave behind. The deep comprehension conveyed here strongly emphasizes how an individual's view of a location changes as they develop a more profound understanding of both them and the world around them.

2. The Revelation of True Fulfillment

The prodigal son's realization comes at his lowest point—when he is destitute and starving. He understands that the fulfillment he sought in a far-off land was always available at home with his father. This parallels the Christian concept of finding true contentment and peace in God's presence. The young man's return to his father symbolizes repentance and reconciliation. Christians can interpret Haig's quote as a call to recognize that ultimate satisfaction and peace lie not in a physical place but in a spiritual relationship with God. The prodigal's journey highlights that external escapes often lead back to the need for internal reconciliation and divine grace.

In the parable of the prodigal son, found in the Gospel of Luke, Jesus tells the story of a young man who demands his share of his inheritance from his father, then squanders it on a life of reckless living in a distant country. However, when a famine strikes the land, the prodigal son found himself in a desperate situation. The famine forced him to take a job feeding pigs, and he even longed for their food. It is in this state of utter destitution that he has a moment of clarity. He realizes that even his father's servants have more than enough to eat, while he is starving. He returns home, not expecting to be received as a son again, but merely hoping to be hired as a servant.

A surprising and overwhelming response greets the prodigal son upon his return to his father's house. His father, filled with compassion and joy, runs to embrace him, and orders a grand celebration to mark his return. His father welcomes the prodigal son back into the family with open arms, and declares, "For this son of mine was dead and is alive again."

People often interpret this parable as a metaphor for the relationship between God and humanity. The prodigal son represents every person who has wandered away from God seeking fulfillment and happiness in worldly pursuits. The prodigal son's desperate realization reflects the understanding that only God's presence brings true contentment and peace. It is a call to repentance and reconciliation, emphasizing the need to turn away from sinful ways and return to a spiritual relationship with God.

This is the true meaning of homesickness. This reminds Christians that a deep connection with God, not a physical place, provides ultimate satisfaction and peace. The prodigal's journey serves as a powerful illustration that external escapes and worldly pursuits often lead back to the need for internal reconciliation and divine grace. In this sense, homesickness truly means longing for a spiritual home, a longing only God's presence can fulfill.

3. Grace and Forgiveness

Upon returning, unexpected grace and forgiveness greeted the prodigal son. His father, filled with compassion, welcomes him back without hesitation, celebrating his return. This act of unconditional love epitomizes God's readiness to forgive and restore those who seek Him. The prodigal son, who had squandered his inheritance in a distant land, realizes the depth of his mistakes and the emptiness of his pursuit of worldly pleasure. He recognizes that his desire to leave his father's house was a mistake, because only God's embrace provides true fulfillment and contentment. Haig's quote, when viewed through this lens, invites reflection on divine forgiveness. The realization that the desired "escape" was unnecessary illuminates the boundless grace available at home—in God's embrace. It underscores the Christian belief that no matter how far one strays, the path back to divine love and acceptance is always open. This powerful story serves as a reminder that no matter how lost or broken we may feel, there is always hope for redemption and restoration in the arms of God.

4. Home as a Place of Transformation

The father's house, which the prodigal initially saw as restrictive and confining, becomes the place of his remarkable transformation. After squandering his inheritance in a life of excess and indulgence, the prodigal son finds himself at rock bottom, desperate and destitute. It is in this state of utter despair that he returns to his father's house, hoping to be treated as a hired servant rather than a son. Little does he know that his journey back home will not only bring him full circle but also lead to a profound inner change.

Open arms and overwhelming love greet the prodigal son as he humbly approaches his father's estate. In this tender moment of reunion, the prodigal realizes the depth of his father's forgiveness and unconditional acceptance. He recognizes the self-destructive path he had followed and the emptiness of worldly pleasures. This newfound wisdom and humility become the catalyst for his transformation.

The prodigal son's story holds a powerful lesson for Christian discipleship. It reminds believers that life's trials and hardships can serve as opportunities for spiritual growth and a deeper faith. Just as the prodigal son experienced a radical change of heart and a renewed commitment to his father's ways, Christians are called to recognize the transformative power of God's love and grace in their own lives. It is through surrendering to God's guidance and embracing the teachings of Jesus Christ that believers can experience true spiritual growth and find their purpose in the world.

The Power of Perception

What we see before us offers an additional layer of insight when considering the prodigal son's story. There is that emphasis on the importance of perception over mere observation, aligning perfectly with the parable's themes.

1. Changing Perspectives

When the prodigal son initially leaves home, he perceives it as a place of limitation and constraint. However, after experiencing hardship, his perspective shifts. He sees his father's house not as a prison, but as a sanctuary of love and forgiveness. This change in perception transforms his understanding of home. In the parable of the prodigal son found in the Bible's New Testament, this story serves as a powerful metaphor for the relationship between humanity and God. It highlights the idea that sometimes we may stray away from God's love and grace, but we can always find our way back to Him. The prodigal son's journey of self-discovery teaches us that home is not just a physical place, but a state of being in communion with God. It reminds us that our true home is in the loving embrace of our Heavenly Father. In a Christian context, this quote encourages believers to look beyond the surface and perceive deeper spiritual truths. Observing life's circumstances is not enough. This parable invites us to reflect on our own lives and consider whether we have strayed from God's path and need to return home. It reminds us that no matter how far we may wander, God's love and forgiveness are always waiting for us, ready to welcome us back into His embrace.

2. Spiritual Insight

The father's reaction to the prodigal son's return further illustrates this point. The father, a figure of unconditional love and forgiveness, exemplifies the core values of the Christian faith. Unlike others who might see a rebellious son deserving punishment, the father sees his beloved, lost child who is now found. His response is not one of anger or retribution, but of overwhelming joy and compassion. This perspective of grace and mercy is central to the teachings of Jesus Christ, who emphasized the importance of forgiveness and reconciliation. Haig's quote challenges us to adopt a similar perspective in our own lives—to see beyond outward appearances and discern the deeper realities of God's love and redemption. It's a call to look with the eyes of faith and recognize God's handiwork in our lives, even in the most unexpected circumstances. By embracing this perspective, we can cultivate a greater sense of empathy, compassion, and love towards others, mirroring the divine nature we are called to reflect.

Conclusion

Combining the quote from Matt Haig with the parable of the prodigal son highlights profound truths about the human experience and the concept of divine grace. Matt Haig's quote delves into the themes of self-discovery, personal growth, and the importance of finding one's true purpose. The parable of the prodigal son tells the story of a son who leaves his home and squanders his inheritance, only to return home humbled and seeking forgiveness.

The journey from escape to homecoming in both narratives symbolize the universal desire for belonging and the yearning to find our place in the world. It speaks to the innate human need for connection and a sense of purpose. The shift in perception from mere observation to deep under-standing signifies the transformative power of returning to God. It implies that by recognizing our own limitations and embracing divine love, we can experience a profound shift in our understanding of ourselves and the world.

The parable of the prodigal son highlights the unconditional love and forgiveness that God extends to all who seek it. In the story, the father wel-comes his wayward son back with open arms, demonstrating the boundless compassion and grace of God. This serves as a reminder that true fulfill-ment lies not in distant pursuits or material possessions, but in the embrace of divine love and acceptance. It suggests that by turning to God, we can find a revelation that has the potential to change our lives and bring about a deep sense of fulfillment and purpose.

In closing, let me share with you a story from my childhood that shaped my perspective and influenced my life's path. As a young child, I was rebellious and struggled to accept parental discipline. Whenever I com-mitted a wrongdoing, I would flee from my parents and seek refuge in the nearby woods, sometimes spending days alone in solitude. During those times, I would sneak back into the house when my parents were at work, grabbing food and fresh clothing to sustain myself. My discontent with their methods of punishment stemmed from their excessive severity. My father, battling his own demons as an alcoholic, would often subject me to merciless beatings. Meanwhile, my mother, feeling embarrassed by my behavior, resorted to using a peach switch from our backyard tree to discipline me. It was a challenging and tumultuous period in my life.

To escape the harsh environment at home, I sought solace in a little laun-dromat in our town. The laundromat had a counter specifically designated for folding clothes, and I would find shelter underneath it at night. Despite the discomfort and constant battle with mosquitoes, it provided me with a temporary sanctuary away from the chaos at home. Hiding from our lone city policeman became a regular occurrence, as I feared the consequences of being discovered.

The impact of these experiences would only become clear to me years later, when I embarked on a journey that mirrored that of the prodigal son. At nineteen, I received a calling to the ministry, which coincided with my work as a Community Worker with Juvenile Court Services. It was during this time that I understood the struggles faced by the probationers I encountered. Drawing from my past, I reached out to them, offering empathy and understanding, hoping they too could find forgiveness and strength to change their futures.

The hardships and challenges of my childhood shaped my passion for helping others and guiding them towards a better path. Through my journey of redemption, I discovered the power of forgiveness and the importance of extending a helping hand to those in need. It is my belief that everyone deserves a chance at redemption, and it is through my experiences that I strive to make a positive impact on the lives of others.

28

The Seed of the Future

❖

I sit on the porch, my fingers delicately cradling a small one-inch seed in the palm of my hand. It is a humble fragment of nature's grand design, hailing from one of the ancient pines that has stood tall and proud around our home for over 75 years. As I examine the seed, I am captivated by its intricate details. A slender wing, a natural marvel crafted by the divine, occupies most of its length, enabling the seed to embark on a remarkable journey through the winds. This tiny seed, so inconspicuous in my hand, carries within it the potential for extraordinary growth and longevity. In the twilight of my life, at 73 years old, I am humbled by the realization that the very pine that produced this seedling predates my existence. It has witnessed the passage of time, silently observing the world around it, rooted in the earth's embrace. It is a testament to the resilience and endurance of nature.

Though diminutive now, I am filled with awe as I contemplate the seed's future. Given the nurturing environment and passing another 75 years, this humble seedling will transform into a majestic pine, soaring ten times taller than my own modest stature. It serves as a poignant reminder that life, in all its forms, holds the promise of growth and the potential to surpass our wildest expectations.

Imagine the trees overreaching purpose by design. With their roots firmly planted in the earth, they serve as nature's guardians, providing shelter, oxygen, and beauty to the world. These majestic beings stand tall and proud, their branches reaching towards the heavens, as if reaching for the sun's life-giving energy. They are the epitome of resilience, weathering storms and seasons with grace. Their leaves flutter in the wind, creating a symphony of rustling sounds that soothe the soul. Not only do trees enhance the aesthetic appeal of our surroundings, but they also play a vital role in maintaining the delicate balance of our ecosystem. Through the process of photosynthesis, they absorb carbon dioxide and release oxygen, purifying the air we breathe.

Their intricate root systems help prevent soil erosion, conserving precious land and protecting against floods. In forests, these towering giants provide a habitat for countless species, fostering biodiversity and supporting the delicate web of life. The timber harvested from trees is a valuable resource that provides us with materials for construction, furniture, and countless other essential products. It is truly awe-inspiring to contemplate the profound impact that trees have on our planet and our lives. They are a reminder of the interconnectedness of all living beings and the importance of nurturing and preserving the natural world.

Imagine all this miraculous creation, from the vastness of the universe to the intricate design of a tiny little seed with its delicate wing. The sheer complexity and orderliness of the natural world leaves little room for doubt—there must be a supreme being behind it all. The existence of such incredible beauty and precision in every aspect of life raises the question: how could this result from mere chance? It is a profound invitation to ponder the existence of a higher power, a creator who has orchestrated every detail with purpose and intention.

In today's fast-paced world, it is easy to become disconnected from the natural environment that surrounds us. However, as an individual who understands the importance of preserving and appreciating nature, I strive to maintain a deep connection with the earth. This dedication extends even to the small and insignificant aspects of the natural world, such as a tiny seed. In this document, I will share a personal experience of finding a suitable resting place for a young seed and the responsibilities that come with nurturing its growth.

Returning to my yard after a long day, I am greeted by the serene ambiance of nature. The vibrant colors of blooming flowers and the gentle rustling of leaves remind me of the intricate beauty that lies within the natural world. As I stroll through the garden, a little seed catches my attention, eager to find a place to grow and flourish. Filled with a sense of responsibility, I decide to provide the seed with a suitable resting place, ensuring its growth in the years to come.

Among the various plants in my yard, I spot a cluster of azaleas. These colorful shrubs, with their dense foliage and vibrant blooms, provide the perfect shelter for the young seed. Carefully, I nestle it between the azaleas, ensuring it is well protected from harsh weather and potential predators. By choosing this location, I aim to create an environment where the seed can thrive and contribute to the overall beauty of my yard.

However, my role as a caretaker does not end with just finding a spot for the seed. As I reflect on the significance of this act, I realize the need to be responsible, attentive, and aware of the natural world around me. Nurturing the growth of a seed requires more than just providing it with a suitable environment. Through this method, one gains a thorough grasp of the plant's needs, including the correct amount of water, the sunlight, and preventative measures to protect it from damaging pests and other potential threats. These responsibilities remind me of the delicate balance that exists within nature and the importance of our role in preserving it.

Cultivating a connection with nature goes beyond appreciating its grandeur; it involves recognizing the value of even the smallest components, like a seed. By finding a suitable resting place for the seed nestled between the azaleas in my yard, I strive to fulfill my responsibility as a caretaker of the natural world. This act serves as a reminder to be attentive to the needs of the surrounding environment. Through nurturing the growth of this seed, I hope to contribute to the overall well-being and beauty of nature, fostering a deeper connection between the earth and all its wonders.

It is a daunting thought, much like that of Johnny Appleseed, that I will never witness this little seed developing into a majestic 75-year-old pine tree. As I hold this tiny seed in my hand, I am filled with wonder and amazement at the immense journey it has ahead. It is as if I am planting the seed of a legacy, a living testament to the passage of time and the beauty of nature's growth.

In my mind's eye, I can already envision the seedling sprouting from the earth, its delicate green leaves reaching towards the sun. I imagine the tree growing taller and stronger with each passing year, its branches stretching out and providing shelter to countless creatures. Birds will build their nests among its sturdy limbs, squirrels will find solace in its protective embrace, and generations of families will gather beneath its shade for picnics and celebrations. The tree will witness the changing seasons, its needles falling, and standing tall and proud against the winter's frost and snow. It will witness storms and calm days, witnessing the ebb and flow of life's challenges and victories.

Though I will never witness this tree's full transformation into a magnificent 75-year-old testament of time, I am filled with a sense of awe and gratitude knowing that I have played a small part in its story. And, in some small way, this little seed will carry a piece of me within its rings, a connection that spans generations and reminds us of all the beauty and resilience of nature.

In the realm of nature's wonders, few phenomena capture the essence of time and legacy as gracefully as the growth of a magnificent tree. As each year passes, a seedling transforms into a towering arboreal giant, reaching towards the heavens in a testament to the enduring power of nature. It is within the realm of this transformative journey that the tale of my great-great-grandson and the awe-inspiring tree he encounters will.

In the distant future, when the passage of time has bridged the generations, my great-great-grandson will stand in the presence of a behemoth, a mighty tree that has stood the test of time. Its grandeur will inspire awe as it stretches skyward, its branches spreading like a welcoming embrace to all who behold it. The colossal trunk, weathered and gnarled by years of growth, will bear the scars of countless seasons, each representing a chapter in the tree's remarkable existence.

The crown of the majestic tree will attract my descendant's gaze as he looks upward, where lush foliage dances harmoniously with the wind. Through the gaps in the vibrant canopy, he will catch glimpses of the boundless skies beyond, a mesmerizing sight that evokes a sense of wonder and curiosity. In that awe-inspiring moment, his thoughts will inevitably turn to the one who planted the seed that set this remarkable journey in motion.

The act of planting a tree, often seen as a humble and mundane task, takes on a profound significance when viewed through the lens of time and generations. It is a gesture that transcends an individual's lifespan, leaving an indelible mark on the world for years to come. The one who planted the seed, a distant ancestor, may have never fathomed the incredible legacy that would unfold from their simple act of nurturing nature.

In the ever-changing tapestry of life, the story of the majestic tree and its encounter with my great-grandson becomes a symbol of the interconnectedness of generations. It serves as a reminder that our actions, even the small ones, have the power to shape the world long after we are gone. As my descendant stands beneath the towering tree, he will embody the spirit of gratitude and appreciation for the one who planted it, recognizing the profound impact that a single act of nurturing can have on the tapestry of existence.

29

The Will of God

—◦◦◦◦—

To start off, let's inquire about what the will of God entails. Theologians, philosophers, and believers alike have pondered the question, "What is the Will of God?" for centuries. The will of God refers to the divine plan or purpose for creation and the guidance and direction that God provides for human beings. It is the ultimate authority and source of moral and ethical principles.

Many seek to understand the will of God through prayer, scripture study, and seeking spiritual guidance. People can see it as a personal and individual journey as they seek to align their lives with God's intentions. People believe that the will of God includes all aspects of life, such as relationships, career choices, and personal decisions. It is a source of comfort and guidance, providing a sense of purpose and direction. However, people also believe that the will of God is mysterious and often beyond human comprehension. It requires faith and trust in God's wisdom and sovereignty. While different religious traditions may have varying interpretations of the will of God, the underlying belief is that it represents God's desire for the well-being and fulfillment of all creation.

In the Bible, specifically in Romans 12:2, the apostle Paul provides guidance on how to live a transformed and renewed life. He encourages believers to not conform to the patterns of this world but to be trans-

formed by the renewing of their minds. This verse highlights the importance of aligning one's thoughts, attitudes, and behaviors with God's truth
and will. Paul emphasizes that this transformation enables individuals to
discern and understand God's good, pleasing, and perfect will for their
lives. Romans 12:2, therefore, reminds Christians to seek personal growth
and spiritual renewal actively through the power of God's Word and the
guidance of the Holy Spirit.

There are three themes in this passage we need to explore to better
understand God's will: nonconformity, transformation, and discernment.
Let us look at each individually.

Nonconformity means that an individual or group intentionally de-
viates from societal norms, expectations, or standards. It is a conscious
decision to resist conformity and embrace individuality. Nonconformists
often challenge prevailing beliefs, values, and behaviors, seeking to express
their unique perspectives and identities. This can manifest in numerous
ways, such as unconventional fashion choices, alternative lifestyles, or unconventional career paths. Nonconformity can be rebellion against social
pressures to conform, allowing individuals to assert their autonomy and
authenticity. It encourages diversity and fosters a culture of acceptance and
tolerance for different ideas and ways of living.

If you say I must close my eyes, bow my head, and kneel to pray properly,
I will argue that it's conformity. I do not feel that those are the requirements to truly pray. One can pray with eyes wide open without kneeling
or bowing the head. When I am in nature, I stand in awe before God's
magnificent creation and offer a prayer.

Prayer is a deeply personal and spiritual experience that transcends any
rigid physical requirements. While some may find solace and focus by
closing their eyes, bowing their heads, and kneeling, it is not a prerequisite
for connecting with a higher power. Everyone has his/her own unique way

of communing with the divine.

For me, being in nature is a profound source of spiritual connection. When I am surrounded by the beauty and magnificence of God's creation, I feel a sense of awe and wonder. Standing tall, with my eyes wide open, I can witness the grandeur of the world around me and offer my prayers with a grateful heart.

Amid towering mountains, tranquil lakes, or vibrant forests, I find solace and peace. Nature's elements become a backdrop for my prayers as I express my gratitude, seek guidance, and pour out my innermost thoughts. There is a sense of freedom and authenticity in this form of prayer, unbound by any physical constraints.

The act of prayer is about the intention and sincerity behind it. It is about opening oneself up to the divine presence and engaging in a heartfelt conversation. The essence of prayer remains consistent, whether one prays with closed eyes, a bowed head, and kneeling, or with eyes wide open, standing in nature's embrace. It signifies a connection to something beyond us.

Transformation in the Christian faith means experiencing a profound change in one's beliefs, attitudes, and behaviors because of a personal encounter with Jesus Christ. This transformation is not simply an external modification of behavior but an inward, spiritual renewal that occurs through the power of the Holy Spirit. It involves a surrendering of one's old self and embracing a new identity as a follower of Christ. Believers in the Christian faith often refer to this transformation as being "born again" or "reborn," symbolizing a fresh start and a meaningful change in one's life journey. It encompasses a deepening relationship with God, a growing understanding of His word, and a desire to live a life that is aligned with His teachings.

Transformation in the Christian faith is an ongoing journey that involves continuous growth, learning, and reliance on God's grace and guidance. It is a process that enables people to find true freedom, purpose, and joy by growing in Christlikeness and sharing His love and truth with the world.

And then we look at discernment. Discernment for the Christian is the ability to distinguish between what is of God and what is not. It involves having a deep understanding of God's Word and being led by the Holy Spirit. Through discernment, Christians can make wise and righteous decisions, avoiding the pitfalls of deception and falsehood. It requires prayer, seeking God's guidance, and relying on the wisdom and discernment that He provides. Discernment is crucial in navigating the complexities of life, facing challenges, and staying aligned with God's will. Developing and honing it is a spiritual gift that comes through a close relationship with God and a commitment to seeking His truth.

In Romans 12:2, the apostle Paul presents a powerful directive to the early Christians, one that remains profoundly relevant today. In this verse, Paul emphasizes the importance of nonconformity, transformation, and discernment in the lives of believers. Paul is urging us to resist worldly values and cultural norms and to present ourselves fully to God. By not conforming to the world's patterns, we set ourselves on a transformative journey towards a renewed mind and a godly lifestyle.

This process of transformation requires discernment, as we seek to understand and align ourselves with God's will. Through the power of the Holy Spirit, we can navigate the complexities of the world and make choices that reflect our commitment to God. Thus, Romans 12:2 serves as a timeless reminder for believers to embrace a countercultural mindset, allowing God to shape and guide their thoughts, actions, and decisions.

The call to remain diligent and faithful to God's call is constant. With the bombardment of the world and its enticements, we do well to humble ourselves before God alone and seek His holy will.

30

"Do Not Be Anxious"

Philippians 4:6 is a verse from the Bible that provides guidance and comfort in times of worry and anxiety. The verse encourages individuals to not be anxious about anything, but to bring their concerns and requests to God through prayer and petition. It emphasizes the importance of a trusting relationship with God, highlighting the fact that He is always present and willing to listen to our worries and provide comfort. By turning to God in prayer, the verse suggests that we can experience a sense of peace that surpasses all understanding, guarding our hearts and minds.

Overall, Philippians 4:6 serves as a reminder to rely on God's strength and seek His guidance during challenging times, finding solace and peace in His presence.

The way we bring our concerns and requests to God through prayer and petition is an integral part of our spiritual journey. Prayer is a means of communication between us and God, a way to express our thoughts, feelings, and desires to Him. It is a powerful tool that allows us to seek His guidance, find comfort in times of distress, and experience His love and presence in our lives.

Through prayer, we can pour our hearts out to God, thus sharing our joys, sorrows, hopes, and dreams with Him. We can present our concerns and requests, knowing that He hears us and cares about every detail of our lives. By laying our burdens before Him, we can find peace and reassurance, trusting that He will provide for our needs and work all things for our good. Prayer is not just a one-way conversation; it is a divine dialogue in which we listen to God's voice and seek His will for our lives. This sacred space, where we can surrender our worries, seek forgiveness, and experience the transformative power of His grace, empowers us for service. Prayer is a way to deepen our relationship with God and align our hearts with His purposes.

Ways that we listen to God's voice include prayer, reading the Bible, seeking guidance from spiritual mentors, and taking part in worship and fellowship with other believers. Prayer is a direct line of communication with God, allowing us to express our thoughts, concerns, and desires while also listening for His guidance and wisdom. Reading the Bible is a way to hear God's voice through His written Word, as it contains His teachings, instructions, and promises. Seeking guidance from spiritual mentors, such as pastors or trusted leaders, can provide insight and discernment in understanding God's will for our lives.

Taking part in worship and fellowship with other believers creates an environment where we can collectively listen to God's voice, as we come together to worship Him, study His Word, and support one another on our spiritual journeys. By engaging in these practices, we open ourselves to hearing and discerning God's voice in various aspects of our lives.

In I Peter 5:7, we read, "Casting all your care upon him; for he careth for you." This verse in the New Testament of the Bible serves as a comforting reminder to believers that they can entrust their worries and concerns to God. The apostle Peter, who authored the book of I Peter, encourages readers to cast their anxieties upon God because He genuinely cares for them. This verse highlights the divine love and compassion that believers can rely on, knowing that they do not have to carry the weight of their burdens alone. It serves as a source of comfort and encouragement, reminding individuals they can find solace in God's care and provision. By placing their trust in God and surrendering their anxieties to Him, believers can experience peace and find the strength to face life's challenges.

In 2 Timothy 1:7, we read, "For God has not given us a spirit of fear, but of power and of love and of a sound mind." his means that we can overcome challenges, face adversity with confidence, and make wise decisions. It is through the power of God's spirit within us that we can tap into our true potential and live a life marked by courage, love, and mental clarity. This verse provides comfort and reassurance for those facing daunting circumstances, reminding them they are not alone and that they have the tools to navigate life's challenges. It is a call to embrace the power of God's spirit and live boldly, knowing that fear does not have a place in our lives.

In summary, followers of faith are to live a life free from anxiety and worry. Through prayer and supplication, we can communicate with God and share our concerns, fears, and desires. In this sacred act of reaching out to our Creator, we not only express our needs but also seek His guidance and wisdom. Amidst the chaos and noise of today's world, prayer becomes our refuge, offering a calm space to listen to His voice and receive divine direction. This powerful tool allows us to align our hearts and minds with God's will, finding solace, strength, and clarity in His presence. In this way, prayer serves as a bridge between the spiritual realm and our everyday lives, offering a source of comfort, peace, and hope.

Sarah, a college student, felt overwhelmed with anxiety about her future. As graduation approached, she struggled with thoughts of not finding a job and financial instability. While attending one of my church services, I spoke about Philippians 4:6. This verse encouraged Sarah to pray and present her worries to God, which helped her release her anxieties. She would share with me later that, over time, she felt a sense of peace and clarity. Interestingly, she ended up securing a job soon after she made peace with her uncertainties.

John, a father of two, received a diagnosis of a serious medical condition. This put immense stress on him and his family. John's wife introduced him to Philippians 4:6, which she meditated on during challenging times. John followed suit and began to pray and express his concerns to God. Miraculously, his health improved, and his family found strength in their faith during this challenging time.

Grace, a high school teacher, often felt bogged down by the daily stresses of her job. The responsibilities of lesson planning, managing a classroom, and grading assignments left her exhausted. Grace remembered her grandmother's advice to turn to Philippians 4:6 whenever she felt overwhelmed. She incorporated this habit into her daily routine, dedicating a few minutes each day to pray and give her worries to God. This practice not only eased her stress but also improved her overall well-being and teaching effectiveness.

What may trouble you today? Take your burdens to the Lord, and He listens, but be sure to hear Him as well.

31

Dots on a Page

M y sister, Jeanette, now eighty-three years old, was born legally blind. My grandmother, who was Jeanette's primary caregiver, raised her until Jeanette lived on her own forty-eight years ago following my grandmother's death. Despite her visual impairment, Jeanette has developed remarkable skills to navigate her modest home. She can faintly see lights and has memorized the layout of her surroundings, allowing her to move around with confidence and independence. Her determination and resilience in the face of adversity are truly inspiring.

Jeanette's educational journey has been nothing short of exceptional. She attended the prestigious Academy for the Blind and graduated with her high school diploma. I have vivid memories of our Sunday visits to grandmother and Jeanette's home, where I would often witness her incredible ability to read using Braille. Braille is a writing system created specifically for the visually impaired, comprising raised dots on a page that form words and sentences. Jeanette would effortlessly interpret those dots and understand the text, leaving me in awe of her intelligence and adaptability.

Though I tried to learn Braille myself, I could never fully grasp the complexity of the system. However, the experience of seeing Jeanette effortlessly read using Braille left an impression on me. It made me appreciate the power of adaptation and the strength of the human spirit in overcoming challenges. Jeanette's journey serves as a constant reminder to never take our abilities for granted and to always seek opportunities to learn and grow, regardless of the obstacles we may face.

The military turned me down for color-blindness because during the examination, I could not identify the letters or numbers on the cards that were shown to me. The cards themselves were a mix of assorted colors, with hidden numbers and letters embedded within them. My color-blindness caused the classification of 4-F, rendering me ineligible for military service. Looking back, I am now grateful for avoiding being drafted into the Vietnam War.

On a fresh note, pointillism is an artistic technique that involves the application of small dots of color in specific patterns to create an overall image. These dots produce a vibrant effect when viewed from a distance, as the viewer's eye optically blends the colors together. Each individual dot on the canvas or page plays a crucial role in realizing this unique artistic effect.

Halftone printing is a popular technique used in the printing industry to reproduce images with gradients and shading. It involves using dots of varying sizes and spacing to create the illusion of a continuous tone. Newspapers and comic books commonly employ this technique to enhance the visual appeal and realism of images. By strategically placing dots of varied sizes and spacing, printers can create a range of tones and shades, making the printed images more visually engaging.

In mathematics, scatterplots are used to represent data points in a two-dimensional space. Each dot on the scatter plot corresponds to a specific data point, with its position on the plot showing the values of the variables being analyzed. Scatterplots are useful for visualizing relationships between variables and identifying any patterns or trends that may exist.

By plotting data points on a scatterplot, it becomes easier to understand the correlation or lack thereof between different variables. The scatterplot provides a visual representation of the data, allowing for a quick and intuitive analysis of the relationship between variables. You can enhance scatterplots with additional visual elements, such as color-coding or different symbols, to represent additional dimensions of the data.

Overall, scatterplots are a valuable tool in data analysis and visualization, providing insights into the relationships between variables and facilitating the interpretation of complex data sets. Professionals in fields such as statistics, economics, and social sciences widely use them to analyze and present data in a clear and understandable manner. By visually representing data points, scatterplots help researchers and analysts make informed decisions and draw meaningful conclusions from their data.

To an astronomer, dots in the evening sky serve as a crucial tool in the process of celestial cartography. By meticulously observing and connecting these dots, the astronomer can map out the intricate patterns and formations known as constellations. These dots aid in determining the movements and distances of stars, unraveling the mysteries of our vast universe. Using telescopes and advanced imaging technology, astronomers can capture the faintest of dots, expanding our understanding of the cosmos and revealing the secrets of distant galaxies. The dots on the celestial canvas provide a roadmap for astronomers, guiding their exploration of the universe and allowing them to uncover new celestial phenomena. From supernovae to black holes, these dots serve as signposts, leading astronomers to new frontiers of knowledge.

Similarly, to a musician, dots on a page hold profound significance as they represent the foundation of a magnificent symphony. When skillfully interpreted and brought to life by the musician, these dots transform into a mesmerizing sequence of musical notes, guiding the audience on an emotional journey from one melodious expression to the next. The dots, also known as musical notation, provide musicians with a universal language through which they can communicate their artistic vision. Each dot represents a specific pitch and duration, allowing musicians to synchronize their performances and create harmonious compositions. Whether it be a complex symphony or a simple melody, the dots on the page serve as a roadmap for musicians, ensuring that their performance is accurate and cohesive.

In both astronomy and music, the dots on a page are not simply random markings, but a means of organizing and conveying information. They are the building blocks that allow astronomers to understand the vastness of our universe and musicians to create beautiful and intricate compositions. Without these dots, the processes of celestial cartography and musical composition would be significantly more challenging. The dots on a page symbolize the intersection of science and art, representing the power of human curiosity and creativity to explore and interpret the world. To the untrained eye, they may not mean much, but to the trained eye, they bring life and meaning and purpose.

Let us now compare those dots and one's faith in God. Individual acts of faith, such as praying, reaching out and helping others, or reading scripture, might seem small by themselves, but together they can transform our faith. Our acts of faith, when viewed together over time, reveal a greater story of our spiritual journey and relationship with God.

Just as each dot contributes to the overall picture, each act of faith contributes to the growth and deepening of our connection with God. These dots, or acts of faith, may appear insignificant in isolation, but when connected, they form a beautiful and intricate tapestry of our spiritual life. Each prayer we utter, each person we lend a helping hand to, and each word we absorb from scripture, adds another thread to this tapestry.

As time goes on, the picture becomes clearer, and our faith becomes stronger. It is through the accumulation of these minor acts of faith that we can truly experience the transformative power of God in our lives. Our spiritual journey is not a single event, but a continuous process of growth and development. Just as each dot is essential in creating a complete image, each act of faith is essential in shaping our relationship with God. Therefore, it is important to recognize the significance of each act of faith, no matter how small it may seem, as it is contributing to the bigger picture of our faith journey.

Creating a detailed image from dots requires patience and trust, even if the ultimate image is not immediately clear. It is like connecting the dots in a puzzle, where each dot represents a piece of the bigger picture. Just as we trust the dots will eventually form a recognizable image, faith often requires trusting God's plan and timing, even when we do not see the immediate results or understand the bigger picture.

Different distances or angles change how we perceive the image. Similarly, our perspective on faith can shift with life experiences, challenges, and insights. Sometimes, when we are too close to a situation, we may struggle to see God's hand at work. However, as we step back and gain a broader perspective, we can recognize the intricate ways in which He is working in our lives. These new insights help us see God's work in new and profound ways, allowing us to deepen our faith and trust in Him.

Connections with others, community worship, and shared experiences also play a crucial role in strengthening and deepening our faith. Just as connecting with other dots in a puzzle helps to complete the overall image, our relationships with fellow believers and our involvement in a faith community provide support, encouragement, and opportunities for growth. Through shared experiences and worship, we not only strengthen our own faith but also witness the faith of others, which can inspire and uplift us.

To tie all these aspects together and guide us in our faith journey, we turn to the scriptures for reference and direction. The Bible is a rich source of wisdom, guidance, and encouragement. In Hebrews 11:1 (KJV), we read, "Now faith is the substance of things hoped for, the evidence of things not seen." This verse reminds us that faith is not just blind belief, but a confident assurance in the promises of God, even when we cannot see them with our physical eyes. It serves as a foundation for our faith, providing us with the substance and evidence we need to continue trusting in God's plan, even when it is not immediately clear to us.

Just as the dots form a complete image when viewed as a whole, our acts of faith collectively build a confident and assured belief in God's plan, even when we cannot see the entire picture immediately. Each act of faith, whether it be praying, trusting in His guidance, or following His teachings, adds another dot to the canvas of our belief. These dots may seem disconnected and insignificant on their own, but when viewed together, they create a beautiful and meaningful image of our relationship with God.

Just as an artist carefully places each dot with intention and purpose, we too must approach our acts of faith with thoughtfulness and commitment. It is through these collective acts of faith that we see the bigger picture of God's plan unfolding in our lives.

Like connecting the dots in a puzzle, each act of faith brings us one step closer to understanding and embracing the divine purpose that God has for us. Though we may encounter moments of doubt or uncertainty along the way, it is important to remember that faith is not about having all the answers or seeing the complete picture immediately. Instead, it is about trusting in God's plan and allowing Him to guide us as we continue to add more dots to our canvas of belief.

As we persevere in our acts of faith, we can find comfort and assurance in knowing that God is working behind the scenes, weaving together the intricate details of our lives to create a masterpiece that reflects His love, grace, and mercy. So let us continue to connect the dots of faith, knowing that each act brings us closer to a deeper and more profound understanding of God's plan for us.

Look for the dots around you today and put your faith into action.

32

Mattresses and Life Choices

❖

Renee, my loving wife, and I recently embarked on a mission to find the ultimate mattress that would cater to our unique needs and provide us with the utmost comfort during our sleep. Given my history of four back surgeries and Renee's early signs of arthritis, it has become increasingly crucial for us to invest in a mattress that offers both firmness and adjustability. Our current mattress, which we have been using for a staggering nineteen years, has unfortunately developed a noticeable wedge in the middle, causing discomfort and disrupting our sleep patterns. As I usually sleep on my side, stretched out, and Renee prefers to sleep in a fetal position on her side, we are determined to find a mattress that accommodates our different sleeping positions while providing the support for our respective health conditions.

Compared to the price we paid nineteen years ago, we were truly astonished by the current, significantly higher cost of mattresses today. We know it sounds crazy, but honestly, we had become quite accustomed to sleeping on that old mattress all those years and, unbelievably, we are planning to keep it and putting it in one of our spare bedrooms, so please do not laugh. It will live on another day!

We discovered the various varieties and prices of mattresses available in the market, ranging from traditional spring mattresses to memory foam and hybrid options. After exploring various stores and testing different mattresses, we came home to have a serious discussion about getting a new mattress. We are not the type of people who make impulsive purchases, especially with something as significant as a mattress. Before making a final choice, we thoroughly contemplate our decisions and weigh all options. We discussed factors such as comfort, support, and durability.

Considering our sleep positions and preferences, we questioned which mattress felt more comfortable. We considered whether the mattress was adjustable to cater to our individual needs. Another important aspect we deliberated on was whether the new mattress would fit seamlessly with our existing headboards and bedroom decor. All these questions and concerns are crucial in ensuring that we make the right decision and invest in a mattress that will provide us with a good night's sleep for the next nineteen years to come. We are both in our seventies, so this may well be our last mattress!

One salesperson at the mattress store gave us an interesting comparison - buying a mattress is like buying a new car. He was determined to provide us with straightforward information. He acknowledged we could explore other options, but he felt compelled to share the "honest" truth about each mattress and its corresponding price. As he bombarded us with questions like, "Do you want it with the pillow top? Do you want the individual controls?", it became overwhelming, to say the least. I was almost tempted to pull out my hair, or what remains of it, because of the sheer complexity of the decision-making process.

Choices surround our daily lives; from the moment we wake up to the moment we go to sleep. We are constantly faced with decisions, big and small, that shape the course of our day. When we wake up, we choose what to wear, what to eat for breakfast, and how we will start our day. Throughout the day, we make choices about how to prioritize our time, what tasks to focus on, and how to interact with others. Even in our leisure time, we face choices about what activities to engage in, what books to read, or what shows to watch. Choices also extend beyond our individual lives and into the broader world. We make choices about the products we buy, the companies we support, and the causes we advocate for. Choices are a fundamental part of being human, and they shape our experiences and the direction of our lives.

Who can we turn to in moments like these to receive the answers we seek? Who can help us make the right choices? The Bible has an answer for that. When facing uncertainty or seeking guidance, we can turn to the timeless wisdom and teachings found within the pages of the Bible. The Bible is a sacred text that is revered by millions around the world as the word of God. It offers profound insights, moral guidance, and spiritual comfort to those who seek it. Within its pages, we can find stories of individuals who faced similar dilemmas and challenges, and through their experiences, we can gain valuable insights and lessons. The Bible provides a moral compass, offering principles and values that can help us make wise and ethical choices in our lives. Whether it is seeking answers to life's big questions, seeking comfort in times of distress, or seeking guidance in decision-making, the Bible can be a source of solace, inspiration, and guidance for those who turn to it.

Scriptures from various religious texts provide us with invaluable guidance on seeking guidance. The Christian Bible, Proverbs 3:5-6, states, "Trust in the Lord with all thine heart; and lean not unto thine own understanding." This verse encourages believers to place their trust in God and rely on His wisdom rather than solely relying on their own limited understanding. It emphasizes the importance of surrendering control and seeking divine guidance in all aspects of life. By acknowledging God's sovereignty and seeking His guidance, individuals are reminded to have faith in His plans and to trust that He will lead them on the right path. This verse reminds us to seek God's direction humbly and to avoid relying solely on our own human reasoning, for true fulfillment and purpose are found through God's guidance.

Similarly, in the Hindu Bhagavad Gita, Lord Krishna advises in Chapter 2, Verse 47, "You have the right to perform your prescribed duty, but you are not entitled to the fruits of your actions. Never consider yourself the cause of the results of your activities and never be attached to not doing your duty." This passage teaches us to focus on performing our duties without being attached to the outcome, emphasizing the importance of surrendering our actions to a higher purpose.

The Quran, the holy book of Islam, provides guidance on seeking guidance through prayer and reliance on Allah. Surah Al-Fatimah, Verse 5-6 states, "Guide us to the straight path - the path of those upon whom You have bestowed favor, not of those who have evoked [Your] anger or of those who are astray." This verse urges believers to seek Allah's guidance in finding the right path and to seek the company of those who have received His favor. These scriptures emphasize the significance of seeking divine guidance and surrendering our actions to a higher power, reminding us that seeking guidance is not only wise but also necessary for leading a purposeful and fulfilling life.

Christian believers have choices about their faith and how they practice it. One choice they have is the denomination they align themselves with. There are various Christian denominations, such as Catholic, Protestant, and Orthodox, each with its own set of beliefs and practices. Christians can also choose how they interpret and apply the teachings of the Bible, with some taking a more literal approach and others adopting a more metaphorical or symbolic understanding. Believers can decide how actively they want to participate in their faith community, whether it is attending regular worship services, joining small groups, or engaging in volunteer work. The choices that Christian believers make are influenced by their personal convictions, values, and understanding of their relationship with God.

The choices we make can have a significant impact on our lives and the lives of those around us. They can shape our personal and professional development, determine our relationships and interactions with others, and define our path towards success or failure. Every decision we make, whether big or small, carries consequences and implications that can ripple through our lives. It is important to approach decision-making with thoughtfulness and consideration, weighing the potential outcomes and considering the values and principles that guide us. Our choices can determine our happiness, fulfillment, and overall well-being. Therefore, it is crucial to make choices that align with our goals, values, and aspirations, ensuring that we are living a life true to ourselves and our beliefs.

Many of us prioritize well-being when making life choices, seeking a fulfilling and comfortable existence. While it is natural to consider material possessions and comfort, such as choosing the right mattress, it is essential to recognize that our life choices extend far beyond these tangible elements. In fact, the way we decide to live our lives has a profound impact on our overall happiness and fulfillment.

1. The Significance of Life Choices:

Our choices shape the direction and quality of our lives. From the smallest decisions to the major ones, they contribute to our growth, development, and overall sense of purpose. Each choice we make influences our relationships, career, health, and personal fulfillment. Therefore, it is crucial to approach decision-making thoughtfully and reflect on the long-term consequences of our actions.

2. Living with Intention:

Living our lives with intention means making choices that align with our values, goals, and aspirations. It involves being mindful of our actions and actively seeking opportunities for personal growth and self-improvement. By consciously shaping our lives in this way, we create a sense of purpose and direction that extends beyond mere material possessions.

3. The Role of Mindset:

Our mindset plays a pivotal role in how we approach decision-making and, subsequently, the quality of our lives. By adopting a growth mindset, we embrace challenges, learn from failures, and actively seek opportunities for self-improvement. Conversely, a fixed mindset can hinder personal growth and limit our potential. Therefore, cultivating a positive and open mindset is crucial for making choices that lead to a more fulfilling life.

4. The Power of Relationships:

Our choices also extend to the people we surround ourselves with. Building and nurturing meaningful relationships can significantly impact our happiness and overall well-being. By choosing to invest in healthy and supportive connections, we create a dedicated support system that enhances our personal growth and resilience. Conversely, toxic, or un-supportive relationships can hinder our progress and negatively affect our mental and emotional well-being.

While choosing the right mattress may contribute to our physical com-fort, it is imperative to recognize that our life choices extend beyond ma-terial possessions. How we decide to live our lives, the values we uphold, the mindset we adopt, and the relationships we cultivate all play a vital role in our overall happiness and fulfillment. By making thoughtful and intentional choices, we can create a life that aligns with our values and aspirations, paving the way for a more meaningful existence.

33

I Have Sworn Off Sports

❧✦❧

Recently, I have stopped watching sports. To me, it feels that the focus on players' salaries overshadows the essence of the game. The focus on financial gain has overshadowed the passion, skill, and teamwork that used to define sports. It's disheartening to see players more concerned about their contracts and endorsement deals rather than giving their all on the field. Exorbitant salaries have created misunderstanding between the athletes and the fans, making it harder to relate to and support them.

The emphasis on money in the world of sports has taken a toll on its integrity and essence. Nowadays, it is common to witness games being interrupted by an overwhelming amount of advertising and corporate sponsorships. This intrusion of profit-seeking tactics has compromised the purity and simplicity that once defined sports. As a passionate sports enthusiast, I yearn for alternative forms of entertainment that prioritize the love of the game over the relentless pursuit of wealth. In a world where money overshadows everything, I long for a return to the true essence of sports, where the focus is on skill, passion, and fair competition rather than the accumulation of riches.

College football, which I grew up loving, introduced a new thing called "The Portal," through which a dissatisfied player can transfer to another team, even a big competitor. Remember that the same player originally committed to their team in a good faith agreement. So, if you are discontent with the way your current team is playing, you simply enter the portal and seek another team. If you are not being played as much as you would like, you can enter the portal. If you dislike the coach or coaching staff, then you enter the portal. This is good for the player but bad for college football and the fans.

Take the Atlanta Braves, one of the most beloved professional baseball teams in the United States. As an avid fan, my allegiance to the Braves dates to their relocation to Atlanta in the late 1960s. I have faithfully followed their journey and supported them through thick and thin. However, recent developments have dampened my enthusiasm. A massive monopoly, which has resulted in an unfortunate consequence for fans like me, has gained the broadcasting rights of the Braves' games. To watch their games, I am now expected to pay an exorbitant price of $150 or more per month. This sudden increase in cost has left me disheartened and unwilling to comply with such an extravagant demand. As a result, I find myself unable to watch my beloved Braves play and connect with fellow fans in the exhilarating atmosphere of live games. It is truly disheartening to witness the transformation of a once accessible and cherished sporting experience into a luxury reserved only for those who can afford it.

It is all about the money! In today's world, financial considerations play a crucial role in every aspect of our lives. From necessities like food, shelter, and healthcare to more extravagant desires such as luxury goods and travel, money determines the quality and options available to us. Money often dictates the opportunities we can pursue, the education we can afford, and the level of comfort we can provide for our loved ones. In the corporate arena, financial success is the goal for businesses, as profits and revenue drive growth and sustainability. In the political landscape, money can be a powerful tool that influences campaigns, policies, and even elections.

Whether or not we like it, money has become an essential component of our society, shaping our choices, aspirations, and overall well-being.

But money can also be our downfall. While it is essential to meet our basic needs and achieve financial security, pursuing wealth can lead to negative consequences. Excessive emphasis on money can corrupt individuals, causing them to prioritize material possessions over personal relationships and ethical values. The relentless pursuit of wealth can create a culture of greed and inequality, where the gap between the rich and the poor widens, and social injustices prevail. The pressure to accumulate wealth can lead to stress, anxiety, and a constant feeling of never having enough. This can negatively affect mental health and overall well-being. Thus, while money can provide opportunities and comfort, it is important to strike a balance and recognize the potential harm it can cause if not managed responsibly.

The Atlanta Braves, a professional baseball team, hold a fascinating origin story that traces back to the visionary mind of Ted Turner. In a bold move that would revolutionize the sports broadcasting landscape, Turner broadcast the team's games on his newly established television station, WTBS, in Atlanta. This decision marked the birth of an iconic partnership between the Braves and the media industry, catapulting the team into the hearts and living rooms of millions of fans across the nation. Turner's innovative approach not only enabled fans to experience the thrill of the Braves' games from the comfort of their homes but also solidified the team's presence in Atlanta's sporting culture. The marriage of sports and media through the Atlanta Braves and WTBS set the stage for a new era in sports entertainment, forever changing the way people engage with their favorite teams. Hank Aaron hit his record-breaking home run there while playing for the Braves.

The moral of this article is to emphasize the importance of staying informed and educated about current events and global issues. Turning the above text into a document suggests that there is valuable information that needs to be shared and documented for others to access and learn from. It encourages individuals to take an active role in seeking knowledge and understanding, as well as promoting the dissemination of information to contribute to a well-informed society. By doing so, we can become more aware of the world, make informed decisions, and potentially work towards positive things. Bring back my Braves!

34

Dust: A Biblical Perspective

C leaning the home is no simple task, and Renee knows it firsthand. She dedicated a solid two hours of her day to rid our humble abode of the notorious dust that seems to accumulate at an alarming rate. As she meticulously wiped down surfaces and vacuumed every nook and cranny, it became apparent that this was not a onetime endeavor. Our home attracts dust particles magnetically. It surrounds us, settling on furniture, floating in the air, and silently infiltrating every crevice. It's a never-ending battle against this persistent foe. Ironically, we realize that the more we clean, the more dust we stir up, creating a vicious cycle of cleaning and re-cleaning. Despite our best efforts, it is an inevitable truth that in just a few short days, Renee will once again find herself armed with cleaning supplies, ready to wage war against the relentless dust.

Since the Bible states we are made from dust (Genesis 2:7), a thought-provoking question arises: could the particles forming our bodies be remnants of our predecessors? This notion opens a fascinating discussion about the interconnectedness of all living beings and the potential continuity of existence throughout generations. Considering the concept of our physical composition originating from dust, it raises intriguing possibilities about the shared origins and shared destiny of humanity. Exploring this concept can shed light on our understanding of our place in the world and the intricate tapestry of life itself.

Dust is a profoundly resonant symbol in Christian theology, illustrating themes of human mortality, humility, creation, and redemption. Let me share with you relevant scriptures to support my premise.

Genesis 2:7: "And the LORD God formed man of the dust of the ground, and breathed into his nostrils the breath of life, and man became a living soul." This scripture emphasizes our humble origins and our connection with the earth.

Genesis 3:19: "In the sweat of thy face shalt thou eat bread, till thou return unto the ground; for out of it wast thou taken: for dust thou art, and unto dust shalt thou return." God was speaking to Adam after the Fall in this passage. It underscores human mortality and the cycle of life and death.

Job 42:6: "Wherefore I abhor myself, and repent in dust and ashes." Dust is often used to symbolize humility and repentance, as seen in the story of Job, where he repents in dust and ashes.

According to Daniel 9:3, the author turned to the Lord God, pleading with prayer, petition, fasting, sackcloth, and ashes. "And I set my face unto the Lord God, to seek by prayer and supplications, with fasting, and sackcloth, and ashes."

This reminds me of the time I stood amid a burned church's ashes and offered a prayer of petition to God to enable our team of volunteers to rebuild and restore what evil people had done to it. A group of individuals, driven by darkness and malice, had targeted a little wood frame country church one fateful night. They set it ablaze, leaving nothing but burned remains in their wake. However, the power of faith and resilience shone through amidst the ashes.

On that solemn Ash Wednesday, our dedicated group of volunteers, fueled by an unwavering determination, gathered at the site of devastation. We stood together, surrounded by the remnants of what once stood proudly, and made a sacred vow. We pledged to rebuild the church, not simply as it was before, but to create a sanctuary that would surpass its former glory. I took ashes from the burned church and made the sign of a cross on each church member's and volunteer's foreheads. This ritual serves as a powerful reminder of human mortality and the need for repentance. With hearts united and hands ready to toil, we embarked on a journey of healing and restoration, guided by the light of hope and the strength of our collective spirit.

This project became a testament to the power of community, faith, and the ability to rise above adversity. And as we worked tirelessly, brick by brick, we witnessed a genuine miracle unfold before our eyes — the transformation of ashes into a symbol of resilience and rebirth. Through unwavering dedication, countless hours of labor, and the outpouring of support from both near and far, the church rose once more, standing tall and strong against the backdrop of the countryside. It became a beacon of hope for all who witnessed its revival, a reminder that even in the face of darkness, goodness and faith can triumph. The rebuilt church now serves as a testament to the strength of the human spirit and a reminder of the power of prayer and unity. The rebuilt church testifies to our collective ability to overcome adversity and rebuild losses.

I was there on the Sunday of the dedication with the church members and witnessed a truly awe-inspiring event. Excitement charged the atmosphere as we gathered to witness the culmination of years of hard work and dedication. The church members transformed the dilapidated, forgotten structure into a magnificent place of worship. As I entered the sanctuary, the overwhelming sense of joy that permeated the air immediately struck me. The sound of hymns being sung with fervor and passion filled the room, lifting our spirits and connecting us to something greater than ourselves.

That day, the preacher delivered a sermon filled with powerful messages of hope, redemption, and God's boundless love. It was as if the very walls of the church resonated with the words spoken, reminding us of the transformative power of faith. As I looked around, I saw the faces of church members, young and old, radiating with happiness and gratitude. We were no longer a group of individuals, but a unified community bound by our shared belief in God's miraculous power and grace.

The dedication of the church was not just a celebration of a physical building but a testament to the resilience and strength of our faith. The dedication stood as a powerful symbol, reminding us that God can bring beauty from chaos, restore the broken, and create new life from despair. It was a humbling experience, witnessing firsthand the transformative work of God in our midst. As I left the dedication ceremony that day, I carried with me a renewed sense of hope and a deep appreciation for the power of faith. The church now stands as a living testament to the extraordinary things that can happen when we surrender ourselves to God's divine plan.

Psalm 103:14: "For he (God) knoweth our frame; he remembereth that we are dust." This verse reflects God's understanding and compassion, acknowledging human frailty and His sovereignty over creation.

Theologically, the concept of being made from dust serves as a reminder of human humility. It emphasizes that, despite human achievements, we remain finite creatures dependent on God's grace and sustenance.

Being formed from dust and brought to life by God's breath also signifies the intimate relationship between humanity and the Creator. This concept emphasizes the profound connection that exists between humans and God, as well as the unique role that God plays in bestowing life upon us. It serves as a reminder of God's active involvement in the creation and sustenance of life, illustrating the depth of His love and care for His creation. This highlights that human beings possess exceptional status because God made them in His image.

This divine image within each individual carries immense significance and sets humanity apart from all other created beings. It implies that humans possess qualities that reflect the divine attributes of their Creator, such as love, creativity, and the capacity for moral reasoning. Thus, the act of God forming humans from dust and breathing life into them not only symbolizes His power and authority but also highlights the inherent dignity and purpose that every human being possesses.

Returning to dust after death also underscores the transient nature of our lives. But Christian theology also teaches that through Christ, there is hope for resurrection and eternal life beyond death, transforming the concept of dust into a symbol of new beginnings and redemption.

Dust, in its simplicity and profundity, continues to inspire reflection of the human condition and the divine relationship that transcends it. From the smallest particle to the grandest celestial bodies, dust serves as a reminder of our humble origins and our inevitable return to the earth. It symbolizes the fleeting nature of our existence, as we are born from dust and eventually turn back into it. This contemplation of our mortality prompts us to question the purpose and meaning of our lives, pushing us to seek a deeper understanding of our place in the universe.

Dust also symbolizes the interconnectedness of all living beings, as we are all made of the same fundamental elements. This unity reminds us we are part of a greater whole, bound by a divine force that transcends our individual selves. Thus, in its simplicity, dust becomes a powerful metaphor for the human condition and a catalyst for introspection, inviting us to ponder the mysteries of life and our connection to something greater than ourselves.

35

Three Key Features of Christianity

❖

I am currently reading a book by Matthew Sleeth, M.D., entitled *Serve God, Save the Planet* (Zondervan, 2007). Matthew Sleeth, a former physician, went through a transformative experience that led him to reevaluate his lifestyle and make significant changes for the betterment of the planet and future generations. Recognizing the urgent need for action, Sleeth embarked on a personal mission to do his part in preserving the Earth. While saving the planet may seem overwhelming for one individual, Sleeth's determination and commitment serve as a remarkable example. His book, *Serve God, Save the Planet*, is a truly inspiring read that has not only resonated with me but also provided the motivation to share my thoughts through this discourse.

Sleeth systematically details three core aspects of Christianity (p. 44), which I aim to elaborate on to enhance our global understanding. He lists these as (1) a personal God, (2) a personal redemption, and (3) a personal accountability. Let's begin.

A personal God and its implication today would mean that individuals believe in a divine being who is not only transcendent but also immanent, actively involved in the affairs of the world and in the lives of people. This belief in a personal God often includes the notion that this divine being possesses qualities such as love, compassion, and the ability to communicate with humans.

Individuals who adhere to this belief may engage in practices such as prayer, seeking guidance or solace from this personal God. The implication of a personal God in modern times is that it offers a sense of purpose, comfort, and a moral framework for believers. It provides a source of meaning and direction, guiding individuals in their daily lives and influencing their values and decisions.

The belief in a personal God can foster a sense of community and connection among believers as they come together in worship, shared beliefs, and a mutual understanding of their relationship with the divine. Overall, the concept of a personal God continues to hold considerable influence and relevance in contemporary society, shaping the lives and worldview of countless individuals.

Various religious texts and sacred scriptures across different faith traditions contain scriptural references to a personal God. In Christianity, the Bible contains many passages that depict God as a personal being who engages in relationships with humanity. For instance, in the Gospel of John 3:16, it states, "For God so loved the world that he gave his one and only Son, that whoever believes in him shall not perish but have eternal life." This verse highlights God's personal love and sacrifice for humanity.

Similarly, in Islam, the Quran describes Allah as a personal God who is compassionate and merciful towards his creation. Surah Al-Baqarah 2:186 states, "And when My servants ask you concerning Me, indeed I am near. I respond to the invocation of the supplicant when he calls upon me." This verse portrays Allah's willingness to hear and respond to the prayers of his followers.

In Hinduism, the Bhagavad Gita portrays Lord Krishna as a personal deity who guides and supports his devotees. In Chapter 9, Verse 22, Lord Krishna states, "I give understanding to those who are constantly devoted and worship Me with love, so that they can come to Me." This verse emphasizes the personal relationship between Lord Krishna and his devotees. These scriptural references affirm the belief in a personal God who actively interacts with and cares for humanity.

A "personal" God is most relevant to us in any culture. The concept of a personal God refers to a deity that is not only transcendent and all-powerful but also intimately involved in the lives of individuals. This idea holds great significance in any cultural setting, as it provides a sense of connection, purpose, and comfort to believers. Humans inherently need a higher power they can relate to personally, regardless of their cultural context. This personal relationship with God allows individuals to seek guidance, find solace in times of trouble, and experience a profound sense of love and acceptance.

A personal God can serve as a moral compass, providing a framework for ethical decision-making and guiding individuals towards virtuous behavior. Whether it is through prayer, worship, or the study of sacred texts, the belief in a personal God offers a source of meaning and direction that transcends cultural boundaries. It is this universal appeal and relevance that makes a personal God significant in any culture.

And friend, have we ever needed a personal God as much as we do today? In an era where societal norms have drastically shifted and our values have become distorted, a personal God can provide us with the guidance and moral compass we so desperately require. Our forefathers, who lived centuries ago, had a distinct perspective on the world, one that was deeply rooted in their belief in a higher power. However, in today's fast-paced and increasingly secular society, the significance of nature, God, and our morals has diminished. A changed moral compass has created an unsettling sense of moral relativism.

The need for a personal God who can provide us with a solid foundation of ethical principles has become more crucial than ever. As the scriptures say, "There is none righteous, no, not one." This acknowledgment of our inherent imperfections and the recognition of our need for divine guidance further emphasizes the importance of seeking a personal relationship with God. By establishing and nurturing this connection, we can navigate the complexities of the modern world with clarity, purpose, and a restored sense of morality.

A second key feature of Christianity listed by Dr. Sleeth is the need for personal redemption. According to Christianity, all individuals are born with a sinful nature and separated from God. However, through the sacrifice of Jesus Christ on the cross, believers can achieve redemption and reconciliation with God. This process of personal redemption involves acknowledging one's sins, repenting, and accepting Jesus as their Lord and Savior. People believe this act of faith saves individuals from the consequences of their sins and grants them eternal life with God. Christian communities emphasize this concept of personal redemption, deeply rooted in Christian teachings.

An old friend of mine used to ask new believers, "Have you been saved since your initial belief?" This question highlights the ongoing nature of personal redemption in Christianity, encouraging believers to grow in faith consistently and strive to live as God's teachings dictate.

The Bible contains many passages that address various aspects of life, faith, and morality. For example, in the book of Matthew 22:37-39, Jesus states, "Jesus said unto him, Thou shalt love the Lord thy God with all thy heart, and with all thy soul, and with all thy mind. This is the first and great commandment. And the second is like unto it, Thou shalt love thy neighbor as thyself." This scripture emphasizes the importance of loving God and treating others with kindness and compassion.

In Proverbs 3:5-6, it says, "Trust in the Lord with all thine heart; and lean not unto thine own understanding; in all thy ways acknowledge him, and he shall direct thy paths." This passage encourages believers to rely on God's guidance and wisdom rather than on their own limited understanding. These are just a few examples of the many scriptures that can provide guidance and inspiration to individuals seeking to live a righteous and fulfilling life.

Dr. Sleeth's third key feature of Christianity is for the Christian to have personal accountability. Personal accountability in Christianity refers to the individual's responsibility to uphold the teachings and principles of the faith in their own lives. It involves taking ownership of one's actions, thoughts, and choices and being accountable to God and to oneself. This concept emphasizes the importance of living a life that is aligned with the teachings of Jesus Christ and striving to be a faithful follower. Personal accountability also entails acknowledging one's mistakes and seeking forgiveness and reconciliation with God and others. A fundamental aspect of Christian spirituality is encouraging believers to examine their thoughts and behaviors continually and actively seek personal growth and transformation in their relationship with God. Personal accountability in Christianity serves as a guiding principle for believers to live a life of integrity, authenticity, and moral responsibility.

Various religious texts and teachings contain scriptures that point to our personal accountability. For example, in Christianity, the Bible emphasizes personal accountability in passages such as Romans 14:12 which states, "So then everyone of us shall give account of himself to God." Another relevant verse is Galatians 6:5 which says, "For every man shall bear his own burden."

In Islam, the Quran teaches personal accountability in verses such as Surah Al-Isra 17:13 which states, "And [for] every person, we have imposed his fate upon his neck, and We will produce for him on the Day of

Resurrection a record which he will encounter spread open."

These are just a few of the many passages that point to our personal roles as human beings in today's world. All three features I have mentioned are most vital to the individual's personal journey through life.

36

Faith Through Adversity

***

Let me begin with definitions of faith and adversity. People commonly understand faith as a strong belief in or trust of something or someone, often rooted in religious convictions. It encompasses confidence, conviction, and a sense of hope. Adversity refers to challenging or difficult circumstances, events, or situations that test one's resilience, strength, and ability to overcome obstacles. It can be personal, professional, or societal, and often presents itself as a setback, a struggle, or a hardship. Adversity can come in various forms, such as financial difficulties, health issues, relationship problems, or even natural disasters. During adversity, faith faces its greatest tests as individuals confront their beliefs, discover inner strength, and depend on their faith to navigate hardship.

The Bible gives us guidelines for each as well. Faith is a fundamental aspect of Christianity, as it is the belief in God and His promises. Hebrews 11:1 describes faith as "the substance of things hoped for, the evidence of things not seen." Faith involves trust and confidence in God's character and His ability to fulfill His promises. It is through faith that we are justified and saved, as the Bible states, "For by grace are ye saved through faith; and that not yourselves; it is the gift of God." (Ephesians 2:8). The Bible also teaches that faith without action is dead (James 2:17), emphasizing the importance of living out our faith through obedience and good works.

Overall, the Bible provides a comprehensive understanding of faith and its significance in the life of a believer.

The Bible talks about adversity in many ways, providing guidance and encouragement to those facing challenging times. The book of James provides one such example, stating, "Consider it pure joy, my brothers and sisters, whenever you face trials of many kinds, because you know that the testing of your faith produces perseverance" (James 1:2-3). This passage highlights the importance of viewing adversity as an opportunity for personal growth and strengthening of one's faith. The book of Psalms contains many passages that express the struggles and emotions associated with adversity. For instance, Psalm 34:17-18 states, "The righteous cry out, and the Lord hears them; he delivers them from all their troubles. The Lord is close to the brokenhearted and saves those who are crushed in spirit." These verses offer comfort and reassurance that God is present in times of hardship and will provide deliverance to those who seek Him. Overall, the Bible provides a rich source of wisdom and guidance for navigating through adversity and finding strength in God's love and provision.

Therefore, the question arises: How does one work through adversity by faith? Adversity is a universal experience that can manifest in various forms, such as personal setbacks, financial struggles, health issues, or losing a loved one. When faced with such challenges, individuals often turn to their faith as a source of strength and guidance. Faith provides a framework for understanding and making sense of difficult circumstances, offering solace, hope, and a sense of purpose. It helps individuals navigate the storms of life, providing them with the resilience and determination needed to overcome adversity. By relying on their faith, individuals can find comfort in the belief that there is a higher power watching over them, guiding them, and providing them with the strength to endure and overcome any obstacle.

Faith can foster a sense of community and support, as individuals come together to pray, share their experiences, and provide encouragement to one another. Through prayer, meditation, and reflection, individuals can find inner peace, clarity, and a renewed sense of purpose. They can surrender their worries and fears, trusting that their faith will guide them towards a brighter future. Ultimately, working through adversity through faith involves surrendering control and placing trust in a higher power, allowing individuals to find strength, hope, and resilience in the face of life's challenges.

The Transformative Power of Adversity

Introduction:

Faced with adversity, individuals often find themselves tested and pushed to their limits. It is during these challenging times they experience a profound transformation, akin to being purged by fire. Adversity can take many forms, such as personal setbacks, professional challenges, or even societal crises. Let me explore with you the significance of adversity in shaping individuals and highlight how these arduous experiences can lead to personal growth, resilience, and a deeper understanding of oneself.

1. Personal Growth:

Adversity has a remarkable ability to catalyze personal growth. Demanding situations compel individuals to confront their fears, weaknesses, and limitations. Through this process, they gain valuable insights into themselves and their capabilities, leading to personal development. For instance, a person facing financial hardship may explore new avenues of income generation, developing financial discipline, and discovering hidden talents. In this way, adversity becomes a transformative force that propels individuals towards self-improvement.

2. Building Resilience:

Adversity is a powerful teacher that helps individuals build resilience. It forces them to confront and overcome challenges, strengthening their ability to bounce back from setbacks. When faced with adversity, individuals learn to adapt, innovate, and find creative solutions. By persisting through challenging times, they develop a sense of resilience that equips them to face future challenges with greater confidence and composure.

3. Discovering Inner Strength:

Adversity has the unique ability to reveal one's inner strength and fortitude. It pushes individuals beyond their comfort zones, forcing them to tap into their deepest reserves of strength and determination. Whether it be battling a chronic illness, navigating through a divorce, or enduring the loss of a loved one, adversity unveils the hidden reservoirs of inner strength that individuals possess. Through these trials, individuals often surprise themselves with their capacity to endure, persevere, and emerge stronger than ever before.

4. Gaining Perspective:

Adversity provides a powerful lens through which individuals gain a deeper understanding of themselves and the world around them. It forces them to reevaluate their priorities, values, and beliefs. By challenging their preconceived notions and pushing them out of their comfort zones, adversity opens doors to new perspectives and opportunities for personal reflection. Individuals often emerge from these experiences with a renewed sense of purpose, clarity, and a greater appreciation for life's blessings.

Adversity, though challenging and often painful, can be a transformative force in the lives of individuals. It has the power to propel personal growth, build resilience, uncover inner strength, and provide a fresh perspective on life. By embracing adversity as an opportunity for growth and self-discovery, individuals can navigate through life's trials with grace and emerge stronger, wiser, and more resilient than ever before.

A notable example of overcoming adversity for the Christian is the story of Joseph from the Bible. Joseph was the youngest son of Jacob, and his father favored him. However, this favoritism caused jealousy and resentment among his older brothers. In their envy, they plotted against Joseph and sold him into slavery. People took Joseph to Egypt, where he faced many challenges and hardships. His accusers falsely charged him with a crime and imprisoned him. Despite his difficult circumstances, Joseph remained faithful to God and maintained his integrity.

Through his unwavering faith and trust in God, Joseph eventually rose to a position of power and became the second most powerful ruler in Egypt, second only to Pharaoh. He could interpret dreams and helped to save Egypt and his own family from a severe famine.

Joseph's story teaches Christians the importance of perseverance, forgiveness, and trust in God, even in the face of adversity. It serves as a reminder that God can bring good out of even the most challenging situations.

I remember a sweet little lady named Mrs. Johnson who lived on the same Georgia hill where I grew up. She was a resilient and determined woman who faced many challenges in her life. Financial difficulties forced her to take on the physically demanding work typically done by men in the community. Despite the hardships, Mrs. Johnson never complained or showed her pain. She worked tirelessly for several local farmers, often enduring long hours and strenuous tasks.

However, her struggles did not end there. Her husband fell ill and required constant care at home for several months. The situation placed additional strain on Mrs. Johnson: she had to shoulder the responsibilities of both parents and care for her two children. To manage the workload, Mrs. Johnson occasionally pulled her children out of school to help her.

One tragic winter night, their house caught fire and burned to the ground. Despite losing everything, Mrs. Johnson remained resilient and determined to keep going. A compassionate neighbor stepped in and offered them temporary shelter in one of his old, clapboarded houses. This act of kindness provided the family with a temporary respite and allowed them to regroup and rebuild their lives.

Mrs. Johnson's story is a testament to her strength and perseverance in the face of adversity. Despite the many challenges she encountered, she never gave up and continued to push forward. Her story serves as an inspiration to all who face hardships, reminding us that with determination and resilience, we can overcome even the most difficult circumstances.

Before I left home for college, I recall seeing Mrs. Johnson one day coming down the hill and walking with her two children arm-in-arm. Though their clothes were ragged, she always skillfully mended them with patches.

I stopped and asked her how things were going. She said, "Honey, I couldn't be better. God has been so good to me! My Billy (her husband) had surgery at the V.A. hospital in Dublin and is back to work. We got another house now near Sugar Creek and love it. Ain't God good?!"

I remember Mrs. Johnson, a devout member of our community, who never missed a Sunday at the Pentecostal Church. Rain or shine, she would be there, radiating a deep sense of faith and devotion. It was a remarkable sight, as I can still vividly recall her raising her arms during worship, surrendering herself completely to the divine presence, and giving passionate praise to God for her salvation. Mrs. Johnson's unwavering commitment to her spiritual journey was an inspiration to all who knew her, and her presence in the church was a testament to her unwavering faith. Her uplifting energy and genuine joy were contagious, filling the sanctuary with an atmosphere of reverence and hope. Mrs. Johnson's dedication to her religious beliefs left an indelible mark on our community, serving as a shining example of what it means to live a life guided by faith and gratitude.

So, you think you've got it bad? Think again. There, but by the grace of God, go you and me. It is easy to get caught up in our own struggles and challenges, convinced that we are the only ones facing difficulties. However, it is important to remember that everyone has his or her own battles to fight. Life is full of difficulties, and no one is exempt from experiencing hardships. Whether it be financial struggles, health issues, or personal setbacks, we all face obstacles that test our resilience and strength. It is in these moments that we must remind ourselves that we are not alone in our struggles.

There are countless others who are facing similar or even more challenging circumstances. This realization should not diminish our own pain, but foster empathy and compassion towards others. By acknowledging that we are all in this together, we can find solace in knowing that there is always hope for better days ahead. So, the next time you feel overwhelmed by your own troubles, remember that there are others out there who are also fighting their own battles. Let this be a reminder to be kind, understanding, and supportive to those around us, for we are all on this journey of life together.

37

Coffeemakers and Change

❦

In the Cravey house, we have been loyal users of Mr. Coffee for 52 years. Since the day we first purchased it, this reliable coffeemaker has been a staple in our morning routine. Over the years, we have never felt the need to switch to a fancier brand or invest in one of those trendy cappuccino makers. The simplicity and functionality of our trusty Mr. Coffee have always been more than sufficient for our needs.

Despite the countless advancements in coffee-making technology, our loyalty to Mr. Coffee remains unwavering. This tried-and-true appliance has consistently delivered a perfect cup of coffee every single time. Its ease of use and durability have made it an irreplaceable part of our daily lives.

Even if the day comes when the company behind Mr. Coffee closes its doors; we are confident that our current machine will continue to serve us well for several more years. In fact, this is not our first Mr. Coffee. Over the years, we have owned and relied on three previous models, each one surpassing our expectations in terms of longevity and quality.

In a world where consumer trends constantly push us towards the newest and flashiest products, our steadfast commitment to our Mr. Coffee may seem unconventional. However, for us, it is a testament to the enduring value of simplicity and reliability. As long as our beloved Mr. Coffee continues to brew our morning cup of joe to perfection; we see no reason to switch to anything else.

There is a sadness and a joy in this metaphor — Life is an intricate tapestry woven with threads of both light and dark experiences. Like a vast canvas, life offers a myriad of emotions and experiences that shape our existence. It is a journey filled with moments of happiness, love, and fulfillment where we find solace and purpose.

Simultaneously, life can also bring forth challenges, heartbreaks, and struggles that test our resilience and inner strength. Just as a tapestry weaves together contrasting colors and patterns, life combines moments of triumph and despair, creating a complex and beautiful masterpiece. Embracing both the sorrow and the happiness inherent in this metaphor, we come to appreciate the depth and richness of life's tapestry, understanding that it is the interplay of light and dark that makes our journey truly meaningful.

Change never comes easy, does it? One day, life is beautiful and sunny; the next, we face dark clouds and a storm. The key to life is to find joy in both. Change is often a good thing, as it allows us to grow, adapt, and discover new opportunities. It pushes us out of our comfort zones and forces us to confront our fears and limitations.

Whether it is a change in career, a change in relationships, or a change in perspective, embracing change can lead to personal and professional development. It enables us to learn valuable lessons, develop resilience, and become more adaptable to the ever-evolving world around us. While change may initially bring uncertainty and discomfort, it can lead to positive outcomes and a sense of fulfillment. It challenges us to question our beliefs, explore new possibilities, and pursue our passions. So, instead of resisting change, let us embrace it with open arms and see the beauty and growth that it brings.

The Bible says that there is a new thing that God is working between Him and you in Isaiah 43:19. This verse states, "Behold, I will do a new thing; now it shall spring forth; shall ye not know it? I will even make a way in the wilderness, and rivers in the desert." Here, God is speaking to the Israelites, assuring them He is about to bring about a remarkable change in their lives. He promises to make a way in the wilderness. He provides streams in the wasteland, showing His ability to bring forth unexpected blessings and deliverance even in the most barren and challenging circumstances. This verse emphasizes God's constant involvement in the lives of His people, revealing His desire to bring about transformation and renewal. It serves as a reminder that God is always at work, bringing forth new opportunities, miracles, and breakthroughs in our lives.

God is all about change. Throughout the Bible, we see many examples of how Jesus brought about a transformation in people's lives. One such instance is when he turned water into wine at the wedding in Cana. This miraculous act not only displayed his power but also symbolized the beginning of a new era. Another powerful example is when Jesus encountered the lame man who sat daily by the Pool of Bethesda. While others ignored his suffering, Jesus compassionately stooped down and healed him, granting him a new lease on life. Jesus showed his unwavering commitment to change by healing the blind, touching lepers, and sending them forth to embrace a brand-new life. These acts of healing and restoration signify God's desire for us to break free from complacency and embrace the transformative power of faith. Jesus constantly challenges us to "get up," step out of our comfort zones, and embark on a journey of personal change guided by his love and grace.

In today's fast-paced and ever-evolving world, the concept of change has become more important than ever. While some individuals eagerly embrace new opportunities and adapt to the shifting dynamics of life, there are others who seem content living in their self-imposed shells, unwilling to step out of their comfort zones. Let us explore the reasons behind this resistance to change, the potential consequences of such a mindset, and the transformative power that lies in embracing change.

1. Fear of the Unknown:

One of the primary reasons individuals choose to live within their shells is the fear of the unknown. Stepping outside of familiar territory can intimidate, as it involves venturing into uncharted waters and facing unpredictable circumstances. This fear often stems from a desire for stability and a reluctance to confront the potential risks and challenges that come with change.

2. Comfort and Familiarity:

Another factor that contributes to this reluctance to change is the comfort and familiarity found within one's shell. Humans naturally seek security and stability, and a comfort zone provides a sense of control and predictability. The fear of disrupting this equilibrium can create a barrier to personal growth and prevent individuals from exploring new opportunities or pursuing their passions.

3. Lack of Self-Confidence:

Some people's fear of change stems from a lack of self-confidence. The uncertainty that accompanies change often raises doubts about one's abilities and capabilities. This lack of belief in oneself can hinder personal development and limit opportunities for growth, leading individuals to settle for a life within their shells.

4. Resistance to Discomfort:

Change often requires individuals to step outside of their comfort zones and embrace discomfort. The resistance to discomfort can be a significant obstacle to personal growth. Many people prefer to avoid the temporary discomfort that comes with change, even if it means sacrificing long-term fulfillment and growth.

Conclusion:

Living within the confines of one's shell is an understandable response to the uncertainties and challenges that change can bring. However, it is important to recognize the limitations and potential stagnation that arise from this mindset. By overcoming the fear of the unknown, embracing discomfort, and cultivating self-confidence, individuals can break free from their shells and embark on a journey of personal growth and fulfillment. Embracing change is not only necessary for adapting to the evolving world, but also essential for unlocking one's true potential and living a fulfilling life.

Not that I am unwilling to try a new coffeemaker. Why should I buy a new one if the one we have still made coffee? I see no reason to invest in a new appliance when our current coffeemaker meets our needs perfectly. It brews a delicious cup of coffee every morning, and its uncomplicated design and functionality have served us well for years. We have become accustomed to its features and know exactly how to adjust the settings to achieve our desired coffee strength and flavor. Our current coffeemaker is durable and reliable, rarely requiring any maintenance or repairs. It has become an essential part of our daily routine, and we have developed a certain attachment to it. Given these factors, it is difficult to justify the need for a new coffeemaker.

One of life's little perks for my wife and me is our twice daily pot of Gevalia Columbian coffee. We have been avid coffee drinkers for years, and we have tried countless brands, but none have matched the quality and taste of Gevalia Columbian. The rich and bold flavor, combined with its enticing aroma, makes each cup a truly delightful experience. Whether it's the first cup in the morning or an afternoon pick-me-up, Gevalia Columbian always seems to hit the spot. The smooth and well-balanced taste leaves a lingering satisfaction that is hard to find with other brands. We have even recommended Gevalia to our friends and family who are fellow coffee enthusiasts, and they too have become loyal fans. With its consistent quality and exceptional flavor, Gevalia Columbian has undoubtedly become an integral part of our daily routine.

We have recently been contemplating the idea of giving up our beloved Gevalia coffee and transitioning towards a more minimalist lifestyle as we enter our older age. As part of this lifestyle shift, we are particularly interested in making conscious choices that promote sustainability and environmental responsibility. One area where we see room for improvement is our coffee consumption habits. Instead of continuing to rely on mass-produced coffee brands, we are eager to explore the world of sustainably grown and ethically sourced coffee. By choosing coffee cultivated using eco-friendly practices, we hope to align our values with our daily indulgences and contribute positively to the planet. If I could only find a variety that is as good as my Gevalia!

Change, embrace it. It will come whether you want it to. It is part of God's new plan for our lives, a divine intervention that seeks to elevate us to new heights of spiritual growth and fulfillment. Don't just sit idly by the pool of complacency but rise from the depths of mediocrity and discover the life-changing power that awaits you. Today, recognize that God is actively leading you towards a profound change - a change in your way of thinking, a change in your way of living, and a change in your very essence. Embrace this opportunity for growth and embrace the path that God has set before you, for it is through change that we can truly unlock our fullest potential and align ourselves with the divine purpose that He has ordained for us. So, let go of fear and resistance, and allow yourself to be guided by the loving hand of God as He leads you towards a life of abundance, joy, and spiritual enlightenment.

38

Green Pastures and Still Waters

—◦◦◦◦◦—

Everywhere I go, whether it's at work, social gatherings, or even in my family, people are overwhelmed with a sense of depression and negativity. The weight of the world seems to rest heavily on their shoulders as they express their concerns and anxieties about various aspects of their lives. Their deep trouble stems from the uncertainty of the future; they constantly worry about what lies ahead and their ability to meet upcoming challenges. Not only that, but they also feel trapped in the present moment, struggling to find joy and fulfillment amidst the daily grind and the constant pressures of modern life. It's as if a dark cloud hovers above them, casting a shadow on their every move. A past filled with regrets, mistakes, and missed opportunities haunts many individuals, weighing heavily on their hearts and minds. It is disheartening to witness the profound sadness and hopelessness that pervade the lives of so many people. It is a stark reminder of the immense toll that life's hardships can take on our mental and emotional well-being.

Depression is a mental health disorder characterized by persistent feelings of sadness, hopelessness, and a loss of interest or pleasure in activities. It affects how a person thinks, feels, and behaves, often interfering with their daily functioning and quality of life. Depression can vary in severity, with some individuals experiencing mild symptoms and others experiencing more severe forms of the disorder. It can also manifest in diverse ways, including persistent depressive disorder (dysthymia), major depressive disorder, postpartum depression, and seasonal affective disorder.

A combination of genetic, biological, environmental, and psychological factors can cause depression. It is important to note that depression is a treatable condition, and individuals experiencing symptoms should seek professional help for diagnosis and treatment options.

Psalm 23 offers one biblical cure for depression. Psalm 23 is a well-known passage written by King David. People often call it the "Shepherd's Psalm," and it offers comfort and solace to those who feel overwhelmed or burdened by depression. In this Psalm, David depicts God as a loving shepherd who provides guidance, protection, and provision for his sheep. The Psalm begins with the words, "The Lord is my shepherd; I shall not want." This declaration reminds individuals they are not alone in their struggles and that God is there to meet their every need. As the Psalm continues, David describes green pastures, still waters, and paths of righteousness, symbolizing God's provision, peace, and guidance.

These images can bring hope and assurance to those battling depression, reminding them that God is present and will lead them through the darkest valleys. The Psalm concludes with a powerful affirmation of God's faithfulness and the promise of dwelling in His presence forever. This message of hope and eternal security can bring comfort to those who are feeling lost or hopeless, providing a sense of purpose and assurance that they are not alone on their journey. Overall, Psalm 23 serves as a powerful reminder of God's love, care, and provision, offering a source of strength and comfort for those struggling with depression.

Green pastures in Psalm 23 refer to the abundant fields where sheep can graze and find nourishment. In this context, green pastures symbolize a place of rest, tranquility, and provision. The imagery of green pastures conveys the idea of God's care and provision for His people, ensuring that they have everything they need for sustenance and refreshment. It represents a place of abundance and blessings where believers can find comfort and restoration. Just as a shepherd leads his sheep to green pastures, God leads and guides His people to places of spiritual nourishment and fulfillment. This imagery serves as a reminder of God's faithfulness and the abundant blessings that He provides for His children.

Still waters in Psalm 23 refer to a metaphorical representation of peace and tranquility. This phrase appears in the well-known biblical passage: "The Lord is my shepherd; I shall not want." The mention of still waters in this psalm signifies the Lord's provision and guidance, creating a sense of calm and rest for those who follow him. Just as a shepherd leads his flock to peaceful streams where they can drink and find refreshment, the Psalmist conveys the idea that the Lord leads and cares for his people similarly.

The imagery of still waters emphasizes the importance of finding solace and rejuvenation amid life's challenges and uncertainties. By trusting in the Lord as their shepherd, individuals can find comfort and serenity, even amid turbulent circumstances. Thus, the reference to still waters in Psalm 23 serves as a reminder of the Lord's faithfulness and his ability to provide a sense of peace in all aspects of life.

I've discovered many accounts suggesting that sheep exhibit an unusual avoidance of drinking water from brooks that produce a soft, flowing sound. Demonstrating his care for the sheep, the shepherd will use rocks to create a contained watering area, banking up the water in a circle so that his flock may drink comfortably and safely. In the same way, as a loving parent provides nourishment for their child, God provides the tranquility and restorative waters that nurture and refresh our souls. He has meticulously prepared a path, smoothing the way for his disciples to follow.

Two other well-known Psalms in the Bible are Psalm 147 and Psalm 148.

Psalm 147 is a hymn of praise that celebrates God's care for Jerusalem and His power over creation. It emphasizes God's healing of the brokenhearted and His provision for those who trust in Him. This psalm also highlights God's sovereignty over nature, as He controls the weather and provides food for all creatures.

Psalm 148 is a call for all creation to praise the Lord. It calls upon the heavens, angels, celestial bodies, and all elements of nature to join in worshiping God. This psalm emphasizes that all created things, from the highest heavens to the depths of the earth, should acknowledge and honor the greatness of God. Overall, both Psalm 147 and 148 express the theme of praising and glorifying God for His faithfulness, power, and creation.

Finally, my favorite Psalm, apart from Psalm 23, of course, is Psalm 46. This Psalm, attributed to the sons of Korah, powerfully conveys trust and confidence in God's protection and strength. People often call Psalm 46 a "song of Zion," and scholars believe it was written during a time of political unrest and upheaval. The Psalm begins by proclaiming that God is our refuge and strength, a very present help in times of trouble. It describes how even if the earth were to give way and the mountains were to fall into the heart of the sea, we need not fear because God is with us. The Psalmist urges us to be still and know that He is God, emphasizing His sovereignty over all nations and reminding us of His coming exaltation on Earth. Verse 10 states, "Be still, and know that I am God; I will be exalted among the nations; I will be exalted in the earth." This verse serves as a powerful reminder to pause, trust in God's plan, and acknowledge His authority and presence in our lives. It encourages us to find peace and solace in Him, knowing that He is in control and will bring about His purposes in His perfect timing.

Looking for green pastures and still waters? Follow the lead of Psalm 23 and Psalm 47:10. Follow the good shepherd, seek the Lord, and He will bless you.

39

Religion in Sociological Perspective

———⋯⋰⋱⋯———

Since the age of eighteen, when I first embraced Christianity, I have found my life deeply enriched by my faith, particularly in the teachings and practices of Christianity and religion more broadly. I held a limited and simplistic worldview, characterized by a naïve understanding of global affairs and a singular, rigid perspective on life's mechanics and the practice of my faith. The prospect of entering full-time ministry terrified me, as my knowledge of the relevant theories, ideas, symbolisms, and rituals was extremely limited, leaving me feeling quite unprepared for the challenges ahead. As a new member of the faith, I often made embarrassing and insensitive remarks, but I always strived to learn and grow from those experiences. In his insightful 1969 work, "Under the Canopy," Peter Berger observed that the wisdom and knowledge necessary for survival are not innate.

Upon completion of my undergraduate studies in Sociology, I continued my education by enrolling in seminary, which led to my earning a Master of Sacred Literature degree. As I began my first day of classes, a theologian, older and of German American descent, sat behind his desk, a pipe in his hand, and immediately, without preamble, declared to the class, "God is dead!" My desire to abandon seminary and return home overwhelmed me, yet an insatiable curiosity to remain and unravel the mystery of God's fate simultaneously compelled me. Over the next four years, I discovered the ploy of the professor. He was merely doing his best to get each student to "think" on such matters and to prove or disprove his theory.

As individuals, we are all actively and independently pursuing answers and resolutions to the questions and inquiries that we each individually possess. The achievement of that goal fosters within each of us a more flexible, open, and inquisitive mindset. In each tiny detail and hidden corner, we relentlessly pursue answers to humanity's most profound and unsettling questions. Berger's 1967 argument centers on the concept of society as a dynamic interplay of opposing forces, emphasizing that this dynamic makes us not merely members of society but also individuals whose identities this dynamic shapes. Our individual actions and beliefs become intertwined with the larger social structure in a reciprocal relationship. In his work, Berger emphasizes three essential and crucial components that are fundamental to this process; these components are, specifically, the processes of externalization, objectivation, and internalization, which are all critical to a full understanding of the subject.

In the process of becoming integrated into society's complex social structures and dynamics, individuals naturally express outwardly, or externalize, facets of their unique identities and internal psychological processes. Objectivation is the process by which we derive benefits from our participation and involvement within the societal framework. Subsequently, we internalize these benefits by consciously integrating them into our awareness, thus starting a cyclical process of continuous improvement and growth.

Berger (page 5) stresses the crucial point that the perpetual cultivation and maintenance of a connection with their respective societies is necessary for humans, who lack innate societal understanding. Thus, we become social creatures, comprising those elements surrounding us and the internalized consciousness of what we have gleaned., society helps to structure humans in our relationships with fellow humans (p.7). This process Berger called "socialization."

Berger talks about *The Sacred Canopy* weakening over time because of the elements of modernization and individualization. This process, which he termed "secularization," involved a complex interplay of social, political, and religious factors. The potential for a decline in religious authority exists, which could weaken the protective structure and established order under which we live and thrive. I believe Berger's overly simplistic study of religion cannot address the multifaceted and intricate nature of the world and its diverse religious experiences. Despite its limitations, it continues to be a tool of significant value within the sociological study of humanity, offering unique insights and perspectives.

Berger's metaphor of the canopy, which represents our shared assumptions, beliefs, and values, creates a sense of stability and predictability in society. Just like the ozone layer that surrounds the earth, this canopy is essential for the proper functioning of society. However, scientists have been warning us about the alarming rate at which we are burning through the ozone layer because of our burning of fossil fuels and the release of harmful gases. As a result, global temperatures are rising year after year, putting society at increasing risk. The potential destruction of this protective layer raises significant societal concerns that we must address more frequently. Unfortunately, some key players, such as oil producers and cattle farmers, deny these claims and contribute to the problem.

It is imperative for sociologists and other stakeholders to act and provide simple answers to this dilemma, rather than simply engaging in endless discussions. The survival of our societal canopy depends on our willingness to confront and tackle these issues head-on. Durkheim, Weber, Freud, and Malinowski give us some basic understanding of how our society functions. Durkheim's discussion of the sacred and Freud's parallel between personal rituals and collective ones, guide us toward taking meanings, symbols, and conception to help us understand the intricacies of our faith and belief systems.

In Weber's *Verstehen*, we discover why we perform specific actions and show empathy to others. It is subjective in how we view others in our society. This attempts to uncover our intentions and what our attached meanings are about. We, as sociologists, may use this approach to help theorize (with empathy) why there are protests or why people dance in the streets carrying signs. What is it that drives them to such activity? As we listen to individuals and corporate groups of people, we soon discover the "verstehen" of why certain things are done.

In his 1907 work, Freud posited an interesting psychological parallel between the rituals we engage in and the neurotic compulsions that frequently plague us. This study served as an exploration into how organizational structures outwardly manifest the shared beliefs and anxieties of the collective. In my profession, understanding individuals, their congregations, and the motivations behind their shared beliefs and anxieties is crucial to helping me comprehend their actions.

In his 2018 work, Malinowski illustrates how religion provides a crucial coping mechanism for individuals grappling with the pressures and emotional burdens imposed by societal structures. His illustrative example of a funeral aptly shows the sociological concept of "social solidarity," highlighting the shared grief and collective response within a community. His extensive study and research on the Trobriand Islanders revealed a fascinating absence of religious rituals amongst the fishing communities who peacefully fished in the calm waters of their local lagoons. However, as they journeyed deeper into the vast expanse of the ocean, their reliance on religious practices grew stronger and more pronounced. I am curious why that is the case. Do our local churches not also practice similar rituals? In times of peace and contentment, we find solace and rest, but when faced with adversity and challenges, we often turn to our faith, sometimes only after exhausting all other options.

In his seminal work, "The Interpretation of Cultures" (2002), Clifford Geertz conducts an extensive exploration into the profound significance and complexities of rituals within the diverse tapestry of human societies. He posits rituals are not simply superficial actions, but deeply concentrated behaviors imbued with profound meaning, significantly influencing our fundamental concepts and the very structure of our existence. Geertz emphasizes the role of rituals in reinforcing social bonds and creating a sense of community, even if they may seem simplistic. He asserts that our moods and meditations are integral concepts that shape our identity and contribute to the development of our spiritual consciousness, both at an individual and collective level.

To illustrate his point, Geertz provides an intriguing example of a Rangda-Barong encounter he witnessed in a local village. During this ritual, the villagers entered a trance-like state, known as "Nadi," where they transcended their ordinary selves and became connected to the realm of spiritual presences. Geertz describes a witch, known as Rangda, who played a vital role in this encounter. The presence of the witch instilled a profound sense of fear and awe among the participants, adding a heightened element of intensity to the ritual experience.

Overall, Geertz's analysis of rituals highlights their multifaceted nature and their significance in shaping our understanding of the world and our place within it. He emphasizes rituals are not just empty customs, but powerful mechanisms that help us navigate the complexities of existence and forge meaningful connections with others. I have discovered that religion serves more than just one function or purpose in life. It gives meaning to and purpose to our lives by providing a framework for understanding the mysteries of the universe and our role within it. Religion also plays a crucial role in promoting social unity and stability in an otherwise chaotic world.

Through shared religious practices and beliefs, individuals can form strong bonds and establish a sense of community. This sense of belonging and shared identity can provide a source of comfort and support in times of crisis or danger. Religion provides a set of norms and values that guide and influence our behavior, helping to maintain social order and cohesion.

Besides its social functions, religion also contributes to our psychological well-being. It offers solace and hope in times of distress, providing a source of comfort and reassurance. Religion can serve as a motivating force for positive social change. Many religious traditions promote values such as compassion, justice, and equality, inspiring individuals to work towards creating a more just and harmonious society. However, it is important to acknowledge that religion is not without its complexities and contradictions.

Because technology possesses the immense potential to advance society and improve individual well-being, its capacity to exacerbate existing societal inequalities and create more profound divisions causes careful analysis and implementing proactive strategies to lessen these detrimental effects. Besides the previously mentioned points, it is important to note that individual religious experiences are diverse and can significantly differ, often resulting in internal conflicts and disagreements within religious groups and communities.

Even with the challenges that are presented, the significant role that religion plays in shaping individual and collective identities is clear, providing essential guidance, support, and a profound sense of purpose for many people throughout their lives. Bender, Cadge, Levitt, and Smilde's groundbreaking and insightful 2012 research profoundly impacted my perspective, leading me to embark on a far deeper and more nuanced exploration of world religions, a subject I had previously viewed with considerable criticism during my ministerial career.

My background includes education at a school that unequivocally asserted the supremacy of Christianity, leaving no room for the acceptance of any other religion as truthful. These sociologists, through their insightful research and teachings, have broadened my perspective of the study of religions. They have encouraged me to explore not just Christianity, but also other belief systems that are influenced by Christian values or completely unrelated to it.

This exposure to diverse world views have challenged my conventional thinking and has compelled me to delve deeper into understanding their unique perspectives. Through their work, these sociologists have effectively opened the door for me to gain a more comprehensive understanding of various religious stances and their significance in society. To Durkheim (Roberts/Yamane, pp. 41-42) there is a distinguished difference between the sacred and profane. He found that the sacred seemed to be found in "God boxes" such as churches, mosques, etc.

We study sociology through quantitative and qualitative statistical analysis by producing research and interview responses to give us a clearer understanding of social systems. Through survey samples, we derive the answers we are seeking. Control variables help us through this process to have a better understanding of the subject. Content analysis is one method used by studying written documents and texts, spoken words and images, to arrive at a conclusion of thought about a particular system or subject.

Each method mentioned in our textbook has its own strengths and weaknesses. Often, many of these methods are used to arrive at answers we seek. No one method determines a clear picture of where we are going or what we believe. Objectivity and our reliance upon empirical data become the hallmarks of any sociological study.

Phil Zuckerman, in his book "Invitation to the Sociology of Religion" published in 2003, explained why individuals adopt religious beliefs. According to Zuckerman, people become religious because of the influence of their social network, the knowledge they gain through learning, or the teachings passed down by their families. This perspective aligns with the "social learning theory" proposed by Bandura in 1977. Both Zuckerman and Bandura argue religious beliefs are not solely a result of personal introspection or innate inclination, but a product of the social environment in which individuals are immersed. By emphasizing the role of socialization and the transmission of beliefs within families and communities, Zuckerman and Bandura shed light on the sociological aspects that contribute to religious adherence. In today's post-nuclear families, a multitude of belief systems and organizations vie for attention, bombarding these families with their messages and vying for their allegiance. Where to turn, what to believe, who to believe in, are all troubling and overwhelming questions. Religion and its teachings are first imprinted on us through our families.

The four "Bs" of Roberts and Yamane, as presented on page 84 of their work, have significantly shaped and influenced my comprehension of the intricate relationship between religious studies and sociological perspectives. In the words of Matthew Loveland (2016), "They are belonging, believing, behaving, and becoming," which speaks to the interconnectedness of these four actions in shaping identity and experience. Everyone needs a place to belong, someone or something to believe in, behave according to societal norms and with societal values, and seek to become what you desire.

Belonging refers to the human need for social connection and identification with a group or community. It gives individuals a sense of purpose, support, and a feeling of being accepted. Believing encompasses the religious beliefs that shape an individual's worldview and provide a framework for understanding the world. It includes faith in a higher power, religious doctrines, and personal convictions.

Behaving refers to the social norms and values that guide individual actions and behaviors within a society. It involves adhering to moral codes, ethical principles, and cultural practices. Last, becoming represents the process of personal growth and development. It involves striving to achieve personal goals, self-actualization, and becoming the best version of oneself.

There are no clear-cut paths to achieve any of these, but, as Berger notes in the Canopy text, we are mammals who were not born with instincts or training like other mammals. We need teaching and nurturing to become the people we hope to be. Therefore, religion and sociology play significant roles in shaping and influencing these aspects of human life.

Religion provides a sense of belonging, offers belief systems, guides behavior, and fosters personal growth, all of which are crucial in understanding the complex relationship between religion and sociology. Last evening I was visiting with my neighbors, a traditional husband/wife and three children. We sat outdoors near dark, and the subject of religion came up. Knowing that I was a pastor, they asked me what I thought about a certain situation happening in the world. Oh, boy! Here we go! I decidedly took off my pastor's cloak and talked to the neighbors from the heart and with the bit of information I have learned.

During our discussion, I thoroughly delved into the first two chapters of Peter Berger's "The Sacred Canopy," a thought-provoking book on the sociology of religion. To my delight, I captivated their interest and sparked their curiosity. Many of my neighbors had never considered the idea that humans are born with nothing, which opened the door to a much deeper discussion.

As we explored this concept further, I drew parallels to the animal kingdom, discussing how dogs, cats, and other mammals are born with innate instincts that guide them to seek food and survive in their environments. This comparison resonated with my neighbors, and it prompted even more profound conversations about the origins of one's faith and belief systems.

It is truly remarkable to witness how a simple conversation, fueled by a bit of knowledge, can have such a significant impact. By engaging in meaningful discussions and sharing insights, we can explore new perspectives, challenge our preconceived notions, and deepen our understanding of ourselves and the world. I am excited to continue these thought-provoking conversations with my neighbors, fostering a sense of intellectual growth and spiritual enlightenment.

40

Lessons From History: Insights for the Future

❖

My father would often say these words of wisdom to me, especially in moments when I had made a mistake or done something wrong. He would gently remind me, "Live and learn, son; live and learn." These simple yet profound words encapsulated a valuable lesson that he wanted me to understand - that life is a journey of continuous growth and learning. Instead of dwelling on our failures or beating ourselves up over past mistakes, my father encouraged me to embrace them as opportunities for personal development and growth. He believed that every setback or misstep was a chance to gain wisdom, resilience, and strength.

By adopting this perspective, he instilled in me a mindset of curiosity, adaptability, and perseverance. Through his guidance, I learned to approach life with an open mind, ready to face challenges, and eager to gain new knowledge. My father's words guided me, shaping my attitude toward success and failure. They taught me to view every experience as a learning opportunity.

We learn from our experiences, whether they are failures or successes. Our past provides valuable lessons and insights that shape our present and future actions. Failures serve as powerful teachers, illuminating the pitfalls and mistakes we should avoid achieving our goals. They teach us resilience, determination, and the importance of perseverance. Successes inspire and motivate us to continue striving for greatness. They show the rewards of hard work, dedication, and strategic decision-making.

Both failures and successes contribute to our personal and professional growth, guiding us towards becoming better versions of ourselves. By reflecting on our past, we gain wisdom and knowledge that can overcome challenges and seize opportunities in the present and future.

History is a vast reservoir of human experiences, achievements, and missteps. By delving into the past, we can glean valuable lessons that help us navigate the complexities of the present and future. Here are some key insights that history offers us:

- Throughout history, unity and cooperation have often produced considerable progress. The creation of the United Nations after World War II is a prime example of global efforts to promote peace and collaboration. Working together, despite differences, can lead to remarkable achievements and a more peaceful world.

- The fall of successful empires, such as the Roman Empire, often serves as a cautionary tale of the perils of hubris. Overexpansion, complacency, and underestimating challenges contributed to their decline. Humility and vigilance are essential. Continuous evaluation and adaptation should accompany success.

- The Industrial Revolution transformed societies, economies, and even the environment. Innovations in machinery, transportation, and communication reshaped the world. We should embrace technological progress but also remain mindful of its societal and environmental effects. Responsible innovation is key.

- History is full of inspiring stories of those who fought for justice. Examples include the American Civil Rights Movement and the end of apartheid. The human spirit is incredibly resilient. Perseverance and pursuing justice can lead to profound societal change.

- The tragedies of the World Wars remind us of the catastrophic consequences of unchecked aggression and nationalism. It is crucial to learn from past mistakes to avoid repeating them. History offers lessons in diplomacy, conflict resolution, and the importance of maintaining international relationships.

- Visionary leaders like Mahatma Gandhi, Martin Luther King Jr., and Winston Churchill played pivotal roles in shaping historical events. Their leadership styles and decisions have left lasting legacies. Effective leadership can inspire and mobilize people toward positive change. It is important to cultivate qualities like empathy, integrity, and strategic thinking in leaders.

As we move forward, let must carry the lessons of history with us. By understanding and reflecting on the past, we can build a more just, peaceful, and sustainable future. History is not just a chronicle of events; it's a guidebook for humanity. Let us heed its wisdom and apply its lessons to the challenges of today and tomorrow.

When I was in a small-town pastorate, our area experienced a severe hurricane. The hurricane caused widespread devastation, leaving many people without homes or necessities. In the aftermath, the churches and community came together in an incredible display of unity and cooperation. Neighbors helped each other clear debris, local businesses donated supplies, and volunteers set up shelters. This experience taught me the profound impact of coming together and supporting one another in times of crisis.

As a young adult in college, I witnessed the rapid evolution of technology in the classroom. Introducing computers and the internet transformed the way we learned and accessed information. This shift made me realize the immense potential for technology to revolutionize education and communication, but it also highlighted the importance of using technology responsibly and ethically.

I remember back in my college days, a spacious room filled with an array of fascinating machinery housed the only computer available on campus. Towering structures of blinking lights adorned the room, creating an atmosphere of technological wonder. The centerpiece of the room was a gigantic screen and keyboard, which stood as the gateway to a whole new world of possibilities. Each student had the unique opportunity to interact with this mainframe computer at the prestigious University of Georgia in Athens, despite the three-hour journey. We embraced this chance by typing brief messages to the mainframe, eagerly expecting the responses we would receive the following day. Looking back, I can't help but marvel at how incredible and ahead of its time this technology seemed to us. It truly felt like we were witnessing something revolutionary.

Nowadays, it's overwhelming to think about the role computers play in our daily lives. We use computers for everything, from emailing and social networking to countless other tasks. They've become indispensable. It's hard to imagine where we would be without them.

"We've come a long way, baby!" is a popular phrase that symbolizes progress and achievement. It reflects the tremendous advancements and milestones we have reached as a society. From technological breakthroughs to social and cultural transformations, constant innovation and evolution have marked our journey. This phrase encapsulates the collective efforts and resilience of individuals, communities, and nations in overcoming challenges and surpassing limitations. It serves as a reminder of how far we have come and motivates us to continue pushing boundaries and striving for a better future. As we reflect on our past accomplishments, we recognize the tremendous growth and progress we have made, and we look forward to the exciting possibilities that lie ahead.

My grandmother often shared stories of her experiences during the Great Depression. Despite the extreme hardships, she and her family remained resilient and resourceful. They grew their own food, made their own clothes, and supported each other through challenging times.

My grandmother would tell me how they turned their backyard into a small garden, cultivating vegetables and fruits to sustain their family. They canned and preserved the excess produce to have food during the winter months. She also mentioned how her mother would sew and mend clothes, repurposing old garments to make new ones. They would trade with neighbors and friends for essentials they couldn't produce themselves. Despite the scarcity of resources, my grandmother's family found creative ways to make ends meet and survive.

Beyond the practical skills they gained, it was their unwavering determination and sense of community that truly inspired me. The stories of perseverance and hope in the face of adversity taught me the importance of staying strong and finding solutions, even in the most challenging situations. Our history has a way of doing that.

During my years of mission work, I had the chance to immerse myself in diverse cultures and engage with people from around the world. This experience broadened my perspective, challenged my assumptions, and enriched my understanding of global issues. It reinforced the importance of cultural exchange and the benefits of learning from diverse viewpoints. Live and learn, son.

As we move forward in the 21st century, with rapid advancements in technology, globalization, and interconnectedness, it becomes imperative for us to carry the lessons of history with us. By delving into the past, we gain valuable insights and perspectives that can guide our actions and decisions in the present and shape a better future. History is not merely a record of dates and events; it is a treasure trove of experiences, struggles, and triumphs that can offer us profound wisdom and understanding. By studying the successes and failures of our ancestors, we can avoid repeating their mistakes and instead strive towards a more just, peaceful, and sustainable world.

History teaches us the importance of empathy, compassion, and respect for diversity. It reminds us of the consequences of discrimination, prejudice, and intolerance, urging us to foster inclusivity and equality. Through historical analysis, we can identify the root causes of conflicts, wars, and injustices, enabling us to find peaceful resolutions and prevent future atrocities. History reveals the power of collective action and the impact of social movements, inspiring us to stand up for human rights, democracy, and social justice.

Besides its moral lessons, history provides us with practical knowledge and expertise. By examining the successes and failures of past civilizations, societies, and economies, we can gain insights into effective governance, sustainable development, and fair distribution of resources. Historical patterns and trends help us expect potential challenges and devise strategies to address them. By understanding the mistakes and achievements of our predecessors, we can innovate and build upon their accomplishments, accelerating progress and fostering sustainable growth.

As we face pressing global issues, such as climate change, inequality, poverty, and political instability, history serves as a guidebook for humanity. It empowers us to make informed decisions, grounded in the collective wisdom of generations before us. By heeding the lessons of history, we can navigate the complexities of our time and work towards a future that upholds the principles of justice, peace, and sustainability. Let us embrace the invaluable knowledge that history offers and apply its teachings to the challenges of today and tomorrow.

Afterword

Other books by the author may be found at Amazon, Books-a-Million, or your favorite bookseller. You may also find several at https://www.drchar lescravey.com.

You may reach the author by email at drrev@msn.com or craveyce@g mail.com.

www.ingramcontent.com/pod-product-compliance
Lightning Source LLC
LaVergne TN
LVHW011219080426
835509LV00005B/220